THE FISHING COMPANION

Lesley Crawford

A THINK BOOK FOR

ROBSON BOOKS

THE COMPANION SERIES: COLLECT THEM ALL

The Birdwatcher's Companion
by Malcolm Tait and Olive Tayler

The Cook's Companion
by Jo Swinnerton

The Countryside Companion
by Malcolm Tait and Olive Tayler

The Fishing Companion
by Lesley Crawford

The Gardener's Companion
by Vicky Bamforth

The Golfer's Companion
by Chris Martin

The History of Britain Companion
by Jo Swinnerton

The Ideas Companion
by Johnny Acton

The Legal Companion
by Vincent Powell

The Literary Companion
by Emma Jones

The London Companion
by Jo Swinnerton

The Moviegoer's Companion
by Rhiannon Guy

The Politics Companion
Edited by Daisy Sampson

The Sailing Companion
by Miles Kendall

The Shakespeare Companion
by Emma Jones and Rhiannon Guy

The Traveller's Companion
by Georgina Newbery and Rhiannon Guy

The Walker's Companion
by Malcolm Tait

The Wildlife Companion
by Malcolm Tait and Olive Tayler

SERIES EDITORS

Malcolm Tait, Emma Jones, Jo Swinnerton
and Rhiannon Guy

Many go fishing all their lives without really knowing it is not fish they are after.

HD Thoreau

THINK

A Think Book
for Robson Books

First published in Great Britain in 2005 by
Robson Books
The Chrysalis Building, Bramley Road, London W10 6SP

An imprint of **Chrysalis** Books Group plc

Edited by Lesley Crawford
Companion team: Tilly Boulter, James Collins, Rhiannon Guy, Emma Jones,
Lou Millward, Matt Packer, Sonja Patel, Jo Swinnerton and Malcolm Tait

Think Publishing
The Pall Mall Deposit
124-128 Barlby Road, London W10 6BL
www.thinkpublishing.co.uk

ISBN 1-86105-919-1

Printed in Italy

The charm of fishing is that it is the pursuit of what is elusive but obtainable, a perpetual series of occasions for hope.

John Buchan

Thanks to the following who gillied so well:
Margaret Buxton; Ewan, Andrew, Ron, Bea and Betty 'Spike'
Crawford; Hazel Mendonca; Howard Montague;
and all the thinkers at Think Publishing.

INTRODUCTION

Angling has, without a doubt, the largest library of any sport.
Since Dame Juliana and her much analysed work of 1496,
The Treatyse of Fyshynge with an Angle, its good disciples have
churned out many thousands of volumes dedicated to this most
baffling of pastimes. Of course, much of the work is technical –
and some too dull to even mention. But there is another side.
Angling, in its time, has bewitched the likes of Shakespeare,
Shelley and Keats. Wordsworth was known to walk 10 miles
for a decent spot of piking and we all know of Hemingway's
obsession with the sport. Even the last two Poets Laureate were
apt to ramble on about fishing And what of other writers? Surely
no one could fault Ransome, Kingsley, or the brilliant Sheringham.
William Caine and 'BB' wrote great works of literature – but
because they also happened to be books about angling, they
were not recognised as such.

But where do you start when faced with such a vast array of
penmanship? I must admit at this point that I have a library of well
over three thousand angling books, some of which I have even read.
Despite this I return most often to just a few titles, all of them either
anthologies or little curios; books you can just dip into and pick out
the juicy bits. Nothing too taxing. For sheer size and scope there is
Paxman's Fish, Fishing and the Meaning of Life. On a smaller scale,
but probably even better is *The Magic Wheel*, by David Profumo
and Graham Swift. But way out front, in my humble opinion, is the
magnificent *Angler's Weekend Book* by Eric Taverner and John
Moore. Nowhere else have I seen a description of coracle fishing as
'the best means of moving forwards, sideways'. In its pages I first
came across the glories of sniggling and stret-pegging, haltering and
daddy-ruffe. Not to mention the afancg, a Welsh water-monster said
to feed on young and comely maidens.

Since 1938 the *Angler's Weekend Book* has reigned supreme as
a book full of absolutely wonderful trivia. Until now. With *The
Fishing Companion*, Lesley Crawford has come close to pushing it
off its perch. It contains such gems as how to ruin your catch,
cockney rhyming slang for fly casters, unrequited love and salmon
in a basket. Need I say more?

Jon Ward-Allen
Editor, *Waterlog* magazine

UNREQUITED LOVE

In the UK and particularly in Scotland, the unusual and not very endearing term 'baggot' (the equivalent of the male sea trout kelt) is applied to a female sea trout that has been thwarted in love. While all other fish have cheerfully managed to procreate, the poor dear baggot has not been able to spawn and shed her eggs. Baggots are to be found in their natal stream, or in inland freshwater lakes or lochs where they are lingering (probably in a deep sulk) and lying low after the unsuccessful attempt they made at spawning in the previous winter. These fish are sometimes caught by anglers in early spring and, if captured, should be returned live to the water. This is particularly important for continuation of the species, for unlike the male kelt, who often dies after the rigours of spawning, the baggot will usually make a recovery and may go on to reproduce more happily in future seasons.

FISH USED IN HERALDRY

Incorporating a fish into a coat of arms has been common practice in Britain for centuries. Examples of various species seen include:

The dolphin • The trout • The grayling
The pike • The shark • The mackerel
The bream • The carp • The bream
The sparling

FISH WARS

Pirating Patagonians

Not many of us realise that in the seas of Antarctica, the sea bass is known as the Patagonian toothfish. So valuable has this fish become – 10 dollars a kilo or more is common – it has gained the name 'white gold'. Illegal poaching of these sea bass occurs mainly in the rich waters of the Southern Ocean. Despite these seas being covered by the Convention for Conservation of Antarctic Marine Living Resources (CCAMLR), a grim game of cat and mouse is being played out daily with 'pirate' trawlers setting down illegal nets, hauling in a catch and then swiftly racing away from policing navy vessels. The pirates are sophisticated in their methods, registering their boats under flags of convenience, falsifying log books, obliterating the names of their boats, and using radar to evade conservation patrols. With funding for the trawlers' crews and their equipment thought to come from less than ethical business sources, this is a war that may not end soon.

10 *Length, in feet, of the commonest length of rod in use for wild trout fishing in the highlands of Scotland*

EIGHT INVALUABLE FISHING BOOKS

1. *An Angler's Entomology* by JR Harris
2. *Freshwater Fishes in Britain* by Davies, Shelley and others
3. *Natural History of the Highlands & Islands* by Fraser Darling and JM Boyd
4. *The Trout* by W Frost and M Brown
5. *A Dictionary of Fly Fishing* by C McCully
6. *Freshwater Fishing* by Falkus and Buller
7. *The Magic Wheel* edited by Profumo and Swift
8. *The Fly* by Andrew Herd

A BIT FISHY

Anagram
What's on the end of your line?
PELTBRED LIAILY
Answer on page 153.

A LITERARY CATCH

It is hard to analyse one's emotions on occasions such as these, when the fish of one's dreams is snatched, as it were, out of the glass case. One's first impulse is to sit down and cry, but, having left such remedies behind with one's youth, one turns naturally to invective. And here again, there is a difficulty. The same medicine is really not adequate for such varied ills as flies caught in the back of one's coat, barbed wire on one's waders, water in one's boots, a be-trampled landing net, and all the rest. Personally, utterance having failed, I become possessed of a dumb and benumbing energy. I pick up the routine of the day, wind in the line, examine the fly, light a cigarette, and walk slowly off into the blue, conscious only that something has stopped inside and that the wheels of articulate emotion have ceased working. Tragedy is supposed to stun, and that is my experience. I make up for it later.

Harry Plunket Greene, *Where the Bright Waters Meet*

SEXY FISH

In pre-Christian times the Greek fish goddess, Aphrodite Salacia was worshipped by her followers on a special designated day, a Friday. On this day they consumed a large helping of fish and then enjoyed an orgy for dessert. From this Greek goddess's first name comes the English month of April, and from her second name comes the English word salacious. The practice of eating fish on Fridays was continued in the Christian world, though the orgy seems to have been dropped, or at least is not so well publicised.

Great industrial city or 'dear green place' it might be, but lesser known is the fact that Glasgow was first and foremost a salmon fishing hamlet based on the River Clyde. Within Glasgow's coat of arms is the legend:

There's the tree that never grew,
There's the bird that never flew,
There's the fish that never swam,
There's the bell that never rang.

The legend surrounding the 'fish that never swam' concerned a lost ring, given by the King of Strathclyde to his errant wife. The Queen is said to have given the ring to a knight, perhaps a secret admirer, but the King found out and crept up on the sleeping knight and took the ring back. In a fit of pique it is said he threw it into the Clyde. The next day a furious King threatened to put the Queen to death unless she brought him the ring. The gallant knight came to the rescue when he confessed to St Mungo, who dispatched a monk post-haste to the river to catch a salmon. When St Mungo cut open the fish there was the ring.

Outcome: One relieved Queen and one fish that never swam...

MAGIC MERMAIDS

Hallucinations (drink-induced or not), sleep deprivation, sexual frustration and poor eyesight seem to be at the root of most stories connected with those mythical creatures, the mermaids. Let's face it, if you are a fisherman on board a trawler, spending long and arduous days and nights at sea, there may well come a time when you start pining for the company of a beautiful woman, and see things that aren't really there. So it's not surprising that centuries-old tales of mermaids, with supernatural powers abound from one length of the country to the other. At Mermaids Rock on the far eastern tip of Corn-wall, local fishermen are said to have been lured to a watery grave by the sound of singing mermaids. At the other end of the country, fish-tailed damsels are supposed to haunt the rocks of Sandwood Bay on the western shores of North Sutherland. And their eerie presence is not confined to the sea. Black Mere, in inland Staffordshire is said to be haunted by a strange mermaid, as is the pool on Kinder Downfall in Derbyshire. In Scotland, the plunging Corrie Halloch gorge in Wester Ross is also linked to a spooky lady not unlike a mermaid. Exhausted, lonely and tipsy fishermen have a lot to answer for...

What do you mean the prawns are off?

QUOTE UNQUOTE

*You are killing me, fish, the old man thought. But you
have a right to. Never have I seen a greater, or more beautiful
or a calmer or more noble thing than you, brother.
Come on and kill me, I do not care who kills who.*
Santiago, contemplating the marlin in
Hemingway's *The Old Man and the Sea*

COMPLEATLY WALTON

When Isaak Walton wrote the seminal fishing book *The Compleat
Angler* in 1653, he wanted its title to convey that the book contained
quintessential knowledge of all things fishing, which of course it did.
However the word 'compleat' has since fallen into disuse in the UK and
has been replaced by its modern version 'complete'. Fortunately, while
the Brits have let the archaic 'compleat' fall by the wayside, the
Americans have embraced it into their language, and use it freely.
Perhaps another case of the Americans taking something very English
and making it their own ...

WHAT ANGLERS SUFFER IN THE NAME OF THEIR SPORT

Floatitus

This is an odd affliction of the coarse fisher. Take a look at your local canal on a Saturday and there will be many anglers there, struck down in their prime with floatitus. Symptoms for this ailment include an inability to move their eyes in any direction other than staring at the little float bobbing around in front of them. Even when engaged in deep conversation, lighting a cigarette or pouring out coffee their eyes remain transfixed.

COCKNEY CASTING

In fly fishing, different situations on the river call for different methods of casting, here are a few Cockney versions:

Tray Cast – Spey cast
Twitch Cast – Switch cast
Upnose Cast – Overhead cast
Stroll Cast – Roll cast
Beetle Cast – Steeple cast
Bubble Call – Double haul

CASTING OFF

In the *New English Dictionary*, to cast means to shed, throw, direct, spread or transmit. You might therefore think that the cast, that quintessentially artistic action of propelling line and hook upon the water, has been with us since man first went angling. Truth is, it hasn't. The very first rods used were so long and cumbersome that to cast anything with the line tied at the sharp end was, well, nigh impossible. In the seventeenth century Colonel Venables did mention casting a fly, 'Be sure in casting, that your fly fall first onto the water', but this was more to do with simply extending the pole over the river and letting the wind blow the line and the attached fly about on the water surface. It was not until the mid nineteenth century, when reels to store the line on came into vogue, that actual methods of casting began to be recorded. Ronalds, circa 1836, takes the trouble to describe how to propel the fly to the water in a 'uniform sweep or curve' round the head. This description was probably the first on what we now know as overhead casting. From then on, fly casting advanced through switch, steeple, roll, single and double spey casts to name but a few. Casting gurus, instructors and demonstrators for these styles of casting remain in great demand, especially amongst lesser mortals not quite able to so elegantly waft the wand.

FISHY METAPHORS

1. To be in a pretty kettle of fish
2. To have a fish face
3. To be better than a slap in the face with a dead fish
4. To be a cold fish
5. To smell like a fish
6. To have something fishy going on
7. To be told there are bigger fishes in the sea
8. To find he's/she's but a small fish to fry
9. To come across plenty of red herrings
10. To fish for compliments
11. To flounder around
12. To drink like a fish

A LITERARY CATCH

The fishes caught upon the coast are cod, ling, turbot, haddock, skate, whiting, dog fish, mackerel, horn-back, sand-eels and flounders... The cods are commonly at 2d, ling at 5d. and skates at 3d. each. The haddocks are in their greatest perfection in December, and sometimes large enough to bring 2d. each. Seals abound on the coast; and it has been occasionally visited by whales, sharks and porpoises.

Description of Caithness in the *First Statistical Account of Scotland* in 1793-1794

THE WINDOW OF OPPORTUNITY

A fish's eyeballs are not the same as ours. For a start the eyes are on the side of the head and do not have any protective eyelids or eyelashes. This means that some fish species will shy away from bright light, as they cannot blink in the same way we do. Neither do freshwater fish see underwater in the way humans do. If you imagine for a moment you are a little trout finning away in the stream, what you actually see above you is a sort of circular window. It's actually quite a pin sharp area, but it's small; the rest of what you see are reflections from the bottom of the water surface rather like a reflection in a mirror. What the angler has to do is keep his outline out of the clear vision 'window' while getting his fly visible in the 'mirror'. It is thought that this idea of fish vision brought about different styles of angling; for example, an angler casting upstream to a fish keeps his shadow out of the 'window' because he is tucked out of sight behind his quarry. Equally, fishing a sunk (wet) fly allows the fly to pop magically through the 'mirror' and appear enticingly in front of the fish. Well, that's the theory, at least...

*If, as I suspect, trout fishing is somewhat of a disease, then
it is also somewhat of a therapy in itself.*
Tom Sutcliffe, American angler

MAYFLY

'The Mayfly is up!' is a shout that will send trout anglers scuttling from pub to riverbank at a superior rate of knots. Quite simply this is 'the' time to go trout fishing. The usually cautious fish let down their guard while trying to gulp down as many of these protein-packed insects as possible and can be caught relatively easily. Often you will see the few weeks of the mayfly season described as 'Duffers Fortnight' and that about sums it up. British mayflies are also known as green drakes and, with their delicate lace-like translucent wings, they are actually quite beautiful. Although they are given the name 'Mayfly', the bulk of the insect hatch occurs in June, and depending in which neck of the British woods you hang out, the hatch may last anything from two weeks to two months. Although it is normally assumed that mayfly inhabit only English chalk streams with rich lush environments, the flies are much more widespread and are found in numerous northern lochs, particularly those of Caithness and Sutherland.

It is often thought that this much-prized insect requires alkaline water to thrive, but the presence of clay-like mud in the river or lake, firm enough for the mayfly nymph to make a decent burrow for its home, is actually more important. Here the nymph may live for up to two years before rising up through the water. Then with a dramatic splitting of the nymph shuck, finally the adult emerges, struggles for a moment on the surface, as if gasping for air, and then takes flight to the nearest vegetation. The mayfly then spends perhaps two days on land drying its wings, during which time the males will dance in spectacular columns in the hope of attracting a female to mate in their midst.

Ultimately after two long years in a dark burrow and two short days carousing, the mayfly mate, the female sheds her eggs back into the water and the delicate Romeo and Juliets die, falling spent with wings splayed, back on to the water from whence they came. While all this drama is in progress, hungry but incautious trout lay themselves open to attack, especially from the cunning angler who imitates the insects with clever designs of natural fly. Not for nothing is it called the mayfly carnival, a madly exciting time for both anglers and fish.

FLIES WITH INNUENDO

Suspenders

Before you conjure up images of anglers dressed up as if they are about to appear in the *Rocky Horror Show*, this actually refers to a type of fly known as a suspender buzzer. Rather than men clad in fishnet tights the name refers more to the action this small artificial fly makes in the water. A Suspender hangs hook-down, quite literally stuck in the surface film. The fly is tied with a very small bunch of semi-buoyant material at its head, which helps keep it upright in the calm water of the lake. This is to try and imitate a small insect of the *Chironomid* (midge) family and shows the lengths that some anglers will go to get a convincing imitation. Whether the trout register this amount of subtlety, is open to debate.

DISAPPEARING SEA TROUT

In recent years catches of sea trout off the west coast of Scotland have fallen from being prolific in the 1960s to being a shadow of their former glory in the twenty-first century. Although we hear many theories as to their decline – anything from global warming to lack of rainfall gets a look in – it is significant that the fall in catches (in the 1980s and 1990s) coincided with the siting of large industrial fish farms in estuaries through which the sea trout must pass. Sea trout are migratory fish, and as youngsters they leave their native rivers to go to sea in order to feed and grow. The only trouble is that since the 1980s the fish have found an insidious and deadly parasite lurking in their normal sea routes. The clouds of sea lice parasites uncontrollably emanating from the fish farms not only bother the stew pond salmon, but also have destroyed thousands if not millions of young wild sea trout. While pro and anti fish farm scientists bickered for years over whether there even was a 'lice problem' and successive governments refused to admit the fish farms were wrongly sited in the first place, the wonderful Scottish sea trout took a dreadful beating, from which it may never recover.

BUT IS IT ART?

One of the more recent ventures of controversial artist Damien Hirst involved a large, predatory fish. The artist obtained a 14ft tiger shark and suspended it in a glass case in a strong solution of limpid green formaldehyde. While you might be forgiven for thinking there is little artistic value in a dead fish, and a protected one at that, left mouth agape dangling forlornly in a bucket of preserving fluid, American billionaire Steven Cohen obviously saw merit in it. In 2005 he paid a cool $8 million to have Hirst's piece swimming in his own art collection.

There are many sayings associated with trout fishing, some more useful than others. Here are a few examples:

1. **Bright day, bright fly** – This is an old maxim about choosing a twinkly bright fly with silver or gold body and/or rib, on a day when there is bright sunshine. The idea is that the fish will spot something flashing in the sunlight and seize it vigorously. Verdict: sometimes works but not 100% reliable.

2. **Dull fly, dull day** – This old saying is perhaps more useful than 'bright day, bright fly'. A fish's eyesight is different from ours and fish do indeed see a dark-coloured fly against a dark sky better than the opposite. Verdict: useful ploy and fails to work only if fish are not in your vicinity anyway.

3. **Big rocks, big fish** – This old saying refers to boulders that are semi-submerged in lakes or large rivers. Trout like to use these as shelter from predators and wild weather, and the crevasses between rocks also harbour good food sources like caddis and snails. Verdict: useful but works only if the water itself is reasonably rich, rocky acidic water may not be so productive.

4. **Clear water, big fish** – Clarity of water can sometimes give a guide to the likely size of trout present. Clear water systems that are spring fed from a limestone base provide rich feeding and consequently the trout grow large. English chalkstreams are a good illustration. Verdict: helpful, but check other environmental factors as well.

A BIT FISHY

What do mackerel, dace, trout, minnow
and ruffe have in common?
Answer on page 153.

A STINGING LINE

In Anglo-Saxon days, fishing nets and lines were made out of nettle hemp. The nettles would be gathered in spring or early summer, the leaves removed and the stems would be soaked in water, pulped and then long stringy fibres drawn out and spun together to form a yarn. The process was rather similar to flax or wool spinning, and the resultant hemp was strong and durable. The fishermen would then use their nettle hemp nets to take unsuspecting fish from both sea and river. Whether fish being captured by this ruse ever gave rise to the catch phrase 'caught in a sting' is not known.

---

18 *Weight, to the nearest pound, of the pollack caught off the Dorset coast in 1986. At 18 pounds and four ounces, it is the British record.*

SCOTLAND'S ALL-BUT-FORGOTTEN TWENTIETH-CENTURY FISHING HEROES

V Carron Wellington

V Carron Wellington wrote only one book, which was published in 1952 and was entitled *The Adventures of a Sporting Angler*. In it he records, with huge verbosity but little pomposity, his escapades while fishing in the remoter areas of Scotland. Wellington was an eccentric angler in the Harrison Ford mould; in fact *Raiders of the Lost Ark* could have been modelled on him, except that it would have been called 'Raiders of the Lost Loch'. He is best known for stripping off, clenching his fishing rod between his teeth and swimming out to inaccessible islands on lochs when no boat was available. Despite Wellington's modern-day obscurity, anglers who accidentally pick up a copy of his long-winded book in some dusty corner of an old bookshop might suddenly find they feel compelled to seek out trout in wild remote places, following in the footsteps of Wellington's boots.

WAYS TO RUIN THE CATCH

1. Store in a plastic bag on a hot day.
2. Forget to gut it when you arrive home.
3. Leave it out uncovered overnight for the cat to nibble on.
4. Boil for half an hour in unsalted water with guts in.
5. Boil for same length of time with guts out.
6. Microwave full power for 30 minutes.
7. Any combination of the above.

I'LL BE BACK

It seems there is a distinctly chilly air between fishermen and administrators when it comes to deciding the future care of Californian coastal waters. On the one hand Governor Schwarzenegger has directed his local authorities to establish a string of marine reserves or fish conservation areas along the State's coastline. Such Marine Protected Areas (MPAs) are supposed to be oceanic refuges where all aquatic species can live free from fishing pressure. However, dismayed big game fishermen are now calling such measures draconian, as the sites of the reserves are near the shoreline where the fish stocks are at their healthiest. Anglers also feel that such sweeping 'no fishing' policies advertised on local TV networks are inflammatory and, not surprisingly, a war of words has ensued. Could it be that the illustrious Governor is simply not a fishing fan?

Weight, in kilogrammes, of some of the largest typical specimen pike
caught in the UK

But of all fresh water piracies, desperate, daring, cruel and devilish, is the leistering or spearing with night lights, and being prevented from all other more sportsman-like methods, this the poachers fall upon, and will effect their purpose by, in spite of all the police force that can conveniently be arrayed against them. Leistering can be effected on spawn beds, by two or three individuals, one to hold the torch, another to use the spear. But as, in the use of lights, they have no sufficient protection from a surprise from the bailiffs, the poachers associate in bands of twenties, thirties or fifties (poor fellows, at the season idle, and therefore daring and desperate) from all the districts around, and disguised in rags and blackened faces, proceed like tribes of Indians to the massacre. Rushing to the spawning gravel beds, over which the flaming lights are kindled, behold fifty or a hundred pairs of fish all promiscuously slaughtered in the very act of spawning...

A dozen bailiffs, who have stolen to the spot with a view to prevention, look stupefied while standing on a cliff of a winter night, in witness of such a scene as this, more bewildered than was 'Tam o' Shanter' when viewing the witches dance to the devils piping.

John Younger, *On River Angling for Salmon and Trout*

BIG, BIGGER, BIGGEST FISH

You can describe your prize catch as:
A lunker
A clunker
A beauty
A denizen
A leviathan
A whopper
A specimen
A monster
One for the glass case

ABATE A BAIT

If you have ever wondered whether the term 'bated breath' fits into angling terminology, the simple answer is, it doesn't. Despite the similar sound to that of a baited hook, the term stems from the word abate meaning lessen or reduce. Somewhere along the line the 'a' of abate was dropped and the word 'bate' was born. Shakespeare apparently used it in the *The Merchant of Venice* – 'With bated breath and whisp'ring humbleness'. Over time, the word bate fell into disuse and it is now common to understand bated breath as meaning 'reduced' breathing. In effect, holding on to your breath rather than a fishing rod...

BRITAIN'S FISHING FASHIONS

Welsh night birds

It's a well-known fact that when the Welsh sewin (sea trout) are in the rivers, Welsh anglers only come out at night. This is because to fish during the day is angling suicide; the gin-clear rivers of Wales mean these wary fish see you way before you see them. Even walking along the bank in daytime will result in the fish departing in droves, and that's before you've put the rod up. To cope with this need for nocturnal angling the Welsh adopt certain strategies. To follow in their footsteps, you need to enhance your night vision (a few carrots might help); then you need to develop the knack of surviving on two hours of sleep; and, finally, you must develop a commando mentality of familiarising yourself with every stone, ditch and ledge on the river in daylight so when you fish in darkness, you avoid upending yourself straight into some very cold water.

STUFF THE FISH

These days taxidermy of fish is usually done by taking an exact fibreglass mould of the catch and then having it expertly painted to resemble the real thing. This is one heck of a lot simpler than all that mess with formaldehyde; however, anglers wishing to preserve for prosperity that 'fish of a lifetime' need to observe some preliminary ground rules. First it's important to take pictures of the fish to record its natural colour for future reference by the artist. Fading and discoloration happens quickly once the fish is landed and exposed to the air, so whip out the camera, take snaps from all angles and then cover the fish. A canvas bag wetted inside and then layered with a little wet sphagnum moss is best, but use a wetted plastic bag if needs must.

To ensure the best taxidermy possible for your prize, phone ahead to ask someone to clear a space in the freezer, leave the water at speed and race home. For future reference by the taxidermist, it's advisable to note down a few essential measurements like overall length, circumference of girth and so on. That done, place the fish flat in the freezer still in its cover but without the sphagnum moss which can freeze to the skin and damage it. Next get on the phone to your friendly fish preserver who will then quote you an exorbitant fee, every bit as heart racing as the capture of the fish. Before agreeing a bank busting price, make sure it includes proper post and packaging for your prize.

With any luck several weeks, or months, later the fish is returned to you in exquisitely painted fibreglass form ready to be forever admired on the study wall.

For over 6,000 years the remote Aleut tribe of North Alaska have survived by fishing for the sockeye salmon. They even have the archaeological evidence to prove it. Recent research has unearthed over 300 ancient village sites linking a prosperous community thriving off the proceeds of salmon harvesting. However, this lengthy traditional way of life was placed under threat in early 2005 when the Aleut were told by US environmental groups and the North Pacific Fishery Management Council to cease fishing as they were 'damaging the North Pacific ecosystem'. In addition the Aleut heritage was further being endangered by the flooding of the retail salmon market with cheap farmed fish, effectively putting the Alaskan tribe out of business. The Aleut did not take this lying down however and produced counter evidence that salmon fishing was central to their birthright. According to a report in *The Times* (March 2005), the Aleut produced a mass of archaeological evidence at an Alaska Board of Fisheries meeting, which refuted environmentalists claims that they were damaging the ecosystem. By proving irrefutably that the tribe had been salmon harvesting for thousands of years with no noticeable effect on the environment, the Fisheries Board relented and even extended the salmon season, thereby allowing Aleut ancient traditions to continue.

QUOTE UNQUOTE

The imitation may be Impressionist, Cubist, Futurist, Post Impressionist, Pre-Raphaelite, or caricature. The commonest is caricature. It therefore catches most fish.
GEM Skues, famous angler and pioneer of the upstream nymph

FISH FACTS

1. Fish are intellectual beings capable of higher thought and reasoning.
2. Fish see you coming.
3. Fish show steely determination in ignoring your fly or bait.
4. Fish attach themselves to other anglers' lines out of spite.
5. Fish put their heads up only when they see you packing up and/or leaving.
6. Fish know when you have a stinking hangover from the night before.
7. Fish know when you don't know much about them.
8. Fish go on holiday the same time as you do.

Take me to the river...

FREQUENCE GRENOUILLE 2005

According to the French e-zine *Sea-River*, Le Reseau des Conservatoires d'Espaces Naturels (the network of French conservation bodies), held a major month long environmental exhibition in Spring 2005. The aim was apparently to make the public more aware of the indispensibles that sustain the equilibrium of our planet. These included 'les zones humides, les crapauds, les grenouilles et autre tritons' ('the wetlands, the toads, the frogs and other marine creattures'), which presumably included fish. The event featured guided tours, conferences, films and cartoons for children and exhibitions illustrating the work being done to provide rescue havens for endangered species in different regions of France. However, why frog frequency is so important is anyone's guess...

He Lived at Dingle Bank – he did; –
He lived at Dingle Bank;
And in his garden was one Quail,
Four tulips and a Tank:
And from his window he could see
The otion and the River Dee.

His house stood on a Cliff, it did,
Its aspic it was cool;
And many thousand little boys
Resorted to his school,
Where if of progress they could boast
He gave them heaps of buttered toast.

But he grew rabid-wroth, he did,
If they neglected books,
And dragged them to adjacent Cliffs
With beastly Button Hooks,
And there with fatuous glee he threw
Them down into the otion blue.

And in the sea they sway, they did, –
All playfully about,
And some eventually became
Sponges, or speckled trout: –
But Liverpool doth all bewail
Their Fate; – likewise his Garden Quail.

Edward Lear, *Dingle Bank*

FISH WARS

Sold-off Senegal

For over 20 years the poverty stricken West African State of Senegal benefited from the income generated by leasing out its fishing rights. The waters off Senegal are rich in fish and EU countries snapped up the deals being offered. For a time the arrangement worked well; however the Senegalese did not reckon on the capacity for high tech trawlers to literally 'hoover up' their fish stocks, leaving locals with a greatly depleted natural resource. Little wooden skiffs and punts were no match for the huge industrial trawlers, and the battle was over before it began. In 2002 the exploitation was finally stopped, and Senegal banned EU vessels from fishing their coastal waters. Whether the fish stocks will ever recover remains to be seen.

24 *Weight, to the nearest pound, of the rainbow trout, caught at Hanningfield reservoir in 1996. At 24 pounds and one ounce, it is the British record.*

Ten thousand dollars for me by myself. For that you get the head, the tail, the whole damn thing.
Captain Quint, the leathery fisherman in the film *Jaws*

ARE YOU GOING TO SCARBOROUGH FAIR?

Alhough it is almost forgotten now, Scarborough was once the haunt of leading 1930s socialites and millionaires. Just like Scotland in August, where hunters head for the grouse, Scarborough was on the elite's social calendar for its autumn sea fishing. The Rothschilds went, as did the Astors, and this quiet seaside town gained a huge reputation among the London set – quite simply, it was the place to see and be seen. However the quarry was not the North sea's humble cod or haddock; the gentry were after much bigger game – tuna. Known locally as the 'tunny', wealthy anglers flocked to catch the huge tuna, which in the early 1900s could be caught in the waters off the Scarborough coast. These big game fish came up from the Med, to feed greedily on the bounteous herring shoals to be found off England's eastern coast in the 1930s. 'British' tuna then grew to enormous size, and eye-popping fish of 550lb to 750lb were regularly caught off these shores. From the 1930s until the outbreak of World War Two, big game anglers haunted this shoreline, the most famous of these hunters being a man named Mitchell-Henry. Brought up on tuna fishing in Nova Scotia, he made the crossover to British tuna in 1929 and never looked back. In 1933 Mitchell-Henry caught the British record tunny, a colossal fish of 859lb. He then got into tackle design and became affiliated to that famous tackle dealer, The House of Hardy. Hardys made a special reel for him, with which to fish for tunny, called, naturally enough, the Mitchell-Henry Reel. The reel was unusually big and in ancient sepia photographs of the proud designer standing beside his enormous catch, the device looks for all the world like a small frying pan.

Mitchell-Henry was also one of the founder members of the 'British Tunny Club', an extremely pukka organisation, chock full of lords, ladies, dukes and duchesses. All had a rollicking time chasing big game at sea until war broke out and, coincidentally, the herring fisheries collapsed from over-exploitation. Without the quality of feeding to attract them to cooler northern waters, those tuna that had not been caught abruptly stopped coming up from the Med. By the 1950s the social set had deserted Scarborough as quickly as they had adopted it, and a short-lived but dramatic piece of British fishing history is now confined to a quiet corner of the Scarborough Museum.

Weight, to the neareest pound of the wild brown trout caught in 1996, at Loch Awe. At 25 pounds and five ounces, it is the British record   25

NECESSARIES FOR A DAY'S BOAT FISHING

1. A well-plumped cushion
2. Balaclava-type head gear which covers neck and head
3. A baler for leaks, boat and personal
4. Bits of string, tape and bendy wire
5. Two rollocks
6. Two oars
7. A reliable outboard motor, if there is such a thing
8. Spare fuel for engine
9. Hot libations
10. A non-leaky waterproof that does not truss you up like a chicken
11. A black bin bag (sit on it, put things in it, etc)
12. An anchor with painter
13. Life jackets
14. Spare fuel for self

A LITERARY CATCH

Never go into the water deeper than the fifth button of your waistcoat; even this does not always agree with tender constitutions in frosty weather. As you are likely not to take a just estimate of the cold in the excitement of the sport, should you be of a delicate temperament, and be wading in the month of February, when it may chance to freeze very hard, pull down your stockings and examine your legs. Should they be very black, or even purple, it might be as well to get on dry land; but if they are only rubicund, you may continue to enjoy the water, if it so pleases you.

William Scrope, *Days and Nights of Salmon Fishing in the Tweed*

A FEARSOME GAFF

To non-fishers, making a 'gaffe' means making a blunder of some sort. There is no mistake however, about using a 'gaff' during the course of a fishing day. This piece of fishing equipment is a mean-looking long-handled hook with a needle sharp point. It is used to scoop up a fish caught by line, and at one time was commonly used by gillies to haul out heavy salmon from the river after the angler had played them to a standstill. While in big game fishing notably in the Caribbean, the gaff is still used if the species is worth keeping for its prize winning and/or eating qualities, thankfully in the UK we use more humane methods to land fish. In England and Wales (though not Scotland) the practice of gaffing fish is now banned on all waters.

Length, in centimetres, at which a red sea bream becomes a legal catch in UK seas

ANGLING PLOYS THAT DIDN'T CATCH ON

Professor Peterson's floating chair

The Shetland Museum's photographic archive carries a wonderful picture of a smartly clad angler, complete with what vaguely resembles a pith helmet, fishing in a loch while perched atop a floating chair. The chair legs have been extended fore and aft to accommodate large plastic floats, which appear to be enormous empty jerry cans laid flat on the water surface. Professor Jack Peterson was an avid visitor to the islands in the 1930s. His unusual craft was kept ready for him at the water's edge so he could go afloat as soon as he reached his angling nirvana. However, despite its ingenious design, the traditional Shetland rowing boat won the day and the floating chair sank without trace.

TEN ANGLING AMERICANISMS

American fishermen have their own special language when it comes to referring to fish, tackle and assorted insects, most of which are a bit meaningless to us Brits. Below are a few quaint Americanisms explained:

Stripers	That popular sport fish, the striped bass
No see ums	Tiny insects a trout might eat
Bobbers	Small float and/or a sight indicator when fly fishing
Clousers	Type of artificial fly type, made with inverted hook and large eyes
Mayflies	All olive and mayfly species come under this collective name in America
Flavs	Insect species, full name *Flavilinea*
Crawdads	Small crayfish also known as 'mud bugs'
Hippers	Waders that reach to the hip
Freestone	A type of river with a loose stone and gravel bed
Humpy	Type of artificial fly made with deer hair body

FISH BLOGGING

In keeping with the latest internet craze of blogging, mobile phone company Nokia has launched Fishblog. For technophobes, blogging is basically posting a diary of words and photographs on the internet for your friends to see. Fishblog will apparently take the concept one step further, by dedicating a website exclusively for anglers to share their successes instantly over the web. Fishers can take a picture of their leviathan and then send it immediately to www.fishblog.co.uk so that others can admire their conquest. With fishing such a hugely popular sport, Nokia reckon they could net quite a profit from the venture.

I'll get to the blighters any way I can...

QUOTE UNQUOTE

*Fly fishing... a cheerer of the spirits, a tranquilliser of the mind,
a calmer of unquiet thoughts, a diverter of sadness.*
Henry Wotton, nineteenth-century English angler

FUNKY REDDS FISH

American and British attitudes to recreational fishing during
spawning time are poles apart. The Brits close their fisheries when
fish are in the act of procreation, whereas the Americans carry
right on angling as if spawning were not a vital issue. In fact
anglers across the pond set great store by fishing techniques that
can be used at this time. According to a March 2005 report on
www.yellowstoneangler.com: 'Some big rainbows have moved into
the creeks to spawn. Due to their funky spawning behaviour, spot
fishing has become extremely easy and the fish are less selective
than normal. An egg pattern, fished behind a redd [a nest-like
indentation in the gravel into which the female fish will shed eggs]
can be a very effective technique.' The reporter then warns anglers
to watch where they are walking, and not to squeeze any eggs out
when releasing fish.

It was reported also on the website that there was to be a series
of meetings over the fate of the native cutthroat trout, which is in
severe decline in the Yellowstone region. Could coitus interruptus
have something to do with it?

The Japanese sport of goldfish dipper catching was shaken to the core in 2003 when it was discovered that its national champion had been cheating. Competition is intense in this quaint sport, and around two thousand individual competitors take part in the national event. The idea is to scoop up as many goldfish as possible in three minutes from a small pond. Competitors have to use an officially sanctioned dipper made of rice paper, rather than nylon net. This they must choose in advance from a selection shown to them by the judges. It seems the cheating competitor sneaked in his own dipper made of standard net rather than soggy rice paper and thereby won all the titles in a clean sweep. He was only found out by chance when a spectator played back a video he had made of the proceedings only to reveal a corrupt sleight-of-hand at work. The cheat had hidden the offending device behind a handheld fan, feigning trouble with the heat but actually effecting a dipper swap when he thought no one was looking.

When confronted with the evidence, the goldfish-catching superstar admitted the crime, saying he had simply 'liked the feel' of the illegal dipper. He was stripped of his title, lost out on an all-expenses-paid trip to Hawaii and received a lifetime ban. The Chairman of the National Goldfish Dipper Catching Federation said: 'We want to try and make the competition as fair as possible, so that we don't destroy children's dreams.'

This really is one heck of a serious sport.

A BIT FISHY

Which is the odd one out?
Bustard, bittern, landrail, grouse and dotterel.
Answer on page 153.

FOODY FLIES

Shrimps

While salmon are at sea they are very partial to the odd shrimp. In fact, eating these crustaceans gives their flesh that rich orange-red tone, whereas a diet without lots of shrimp means that the salmon's flesh remains a dull grey-white. Salmon anglers realised this quite some years ago and tied flies that vaguely resembled a darting shrimp, in the hope that seeing the gaudy fly in a river would remind the salmon of their sea-feeding phase. In the 1980s Scotsman Ally Gowans invented a British, if not world, bestselling salmon fly known as 'The Ally's Shrimp'. This fly has a brilliant orange and black hue and has proved irresistible to salmon everywhere.

VIVE LA DIFFERENCE

That doyen of haute cuisine, Georges Auguste Escoffier, once feted the humble pike with a recipe 'Quenelles de Brochet a la Lyonnaise'. Here is the original Anglicised version of his recipe:

Ingredients:
1lb pike meat
1lb beef kidney fat
1lb frangipane panada
4 egg whites

Method: Fillet the pike, remove skin and bones and then pound up the flesh. Make a fish stock with the bones combined with the usual ingredients of white wine vinegar, seasoning, tarragon etc.

Pound up the kidney fat in a separate dish. Prepare panada and then mix up 1lb of this with the four beaten egg whites. Slowly combine the pike meat and the fat to the frangipane mixture and pound all to a smooth paste. Rub through a sieve until a puree with the appearance of forcemeat stuffing is obtained. Leave to cool.

Mould some quenelles from the mixture and then poach them for about seven minutes in boiling salted water. Drain and simmer in some of the fish stock for a further 10 minutes and then combine with whatever sauce you fancy.

ICE ICE BABY

You might think that sitting on ice in the middle of a great frozen lake in the wilds of Alaska or Scandinavia, waiting for a fish to bite, borders on the unconventional if not a bit weird. But then, given that most fishermen and women are slightly mad anyway, this branch of angling should come as no surprise. The fish most anglers are after are usually char or walleye pollack and some big ones at that. Anglers use specially made, tiny fishing rods no more than two feet long, and after drilling a hole in the ice, they then dangle line and bait down in the hope a passing fish will take hold.

There is no casting or bait selection skill required; the most successful anglers are the ones who know where to drill their holes. Expert ice anglers pinpoint fish under the water by methodically drilling test bores around potentially productive areas, such as underwater promontories, or where they know a stream would normally flow in to the lake. In fact the drilling is much more energetic than the fishing itself which is more or less static, and usually jolly sociable with anglers passing round the beer, whisky or schnapps as they wait for a bite. Scotch on the rocks, anyone?

WHEN WHAT YOU SAY IS NOT
NECESSARILY WHAT YOU MEAN

While anglers love to talk when they're out fishing, their conversations may not be quite as innocent as they seem. Here are a few examples of some hidden meanings:

'Caught anything yet mate?' said with deflated demeanour.
Really means: 'I've had a beast of a day and I want you to have had the same so I don't feel so bad.'

'Caught anything yet, mate?' said with perky conviction.
Really means: 'I've caught loads today and I hope you haven't so I can look superior.'

'Do you mind if I fish here?'
Really means: 'Stop hogging all the action'.

'Saw a lot of fish rising in the next bay.'
Really means: 'Don't want your company just now, mate'.

'Old Fred caught 12 today.'
Really means: 'Are you a local? If you don't know Fred, there's not much point in asking you how things are going, because you won't have the home water knowledge.'

'Caught a lot of fish on the [insert name] fly or the [insert name] bait.'
Really means: 'I've caught enough to satisfy my ego; now it's your turn... that's if there's any fish left in the vicinity.'

A LITERARY CATCH

Clean scouring your worms makes them clear, red, tough and to live long on the hook, and to keep colour, and therefore more desirable to the fish: a little Bol Amoniac put to them, will much further your desire, and scour them in a short time: or you put them all night in water, and they will scour themselves, which will weaken them; but a few hours in good moss will recover them. Lest your worms die, you may feed them with crumbs of bread and milk, or fine flour and milk, or the yolk of an egg, and sweet cream coagulated over the fire, given to them little and often; sometimes also put to them earth cast out of a grave, the newer the grave the better; I mean the shorter time the party has been buried, you will find fish will exceedingly covet them after this earth, and here you may gather what gum that is, which J D in his *Secrets of Angling* calls 'Gum of Life'.

Colonel Robert Venables,
The Experienced Angler or Angling Improved

The Battle for Beluga

For a solitary, long-living, non-aggressive fish, the sturgeon is causing mighty serious trouble in the Caspian Sea. Since the break up of the Soviet Union, all hell has broken out, with fishermen from Russia, Kazakhstan, Azerbaijan, Iran and Turkmenistan all competing to catch sturgeon, legally or illegally. The reason is caviar. One giant beluga sturgeon full of eggs can fetch as much as £15,000 on the international market.

Of course the sturgeon has always been exploited for its highly rated eggy delicacies, but in the twenty-first century the problems of overfishing have now reached epic proportions. Poaching from all sides has seen stocks of sturgeon fall to an all-time low, and extinction is looming large on the horizon. Police patrols are constantly trying to stop illegal fishing, sometimes with the aid of bombs, bullets and helicopter patrols. Even when they are successful, local fishermen then accuse the authorities of profiteering by selling on the catch themselves. All in all, not a good time to be a sturgeon.

ENGLAND'S CHANGING CHALKSTREAMS

To the non-angler the sweetly clear meandering streams of Hampshire, Wiltshire and Dorset look as if they have been that way for centuries, when in fact the rivers have been having radical overhauls since time immemorial. According to the Wild Trout Trust, since the fourteenth century, if not earlier, England's tranquil chalkstreams have been altered to meet the demands of industry, water supplies, war and agriculture. First came the needs of the old water mills for flour production, then in the seventeenth century the chalkstreams were reverted to water meadow systems presumably in the name of agriculture. But the environmental shake-up didn't end there, for in the twentieth century the rivers changed in nature again when they were widened and deepened to act as deterrents to any invading German forces. In addition, the surrounding meadows were drained and replanted to facilitate crop-growing to support the war effort. And to cap it all, in the post war era, river abstraction for water supplies began in earnest, accompanied by a general draining of the landscape in the name of flood prevention. While they cannot hope to fully restore natural fish habitats to what they were, especially rivers that have seen so much change over the centuries, the Wild Trout Trust has done and continues to do some commendable work on chalkstream habitats. Find out more about their work at www.wildtrout.org.

Number of fish species present in the River Avon ranging from lampreys to mullets

SUSTAINABILITY AND ALL THAT

Environmentalists are forever telling us that we need a sustainable this and a sustainable that. In fact this buzz word is applied to just about anything animal, mineral or vegetable and of course, it's applied to fisheries as well. So just what is a sustainable fishery? In truth, it is sometimes not that easy to distinguish good from bad, but the conservation-minded angler might want to bear in mind the following:

A sustainable fishery is one where:

- The management and staff know and care about their fish; you'd be surprised how many do not.
- Clear records of catches, including size and weight, are kept.
- Future stocking is planned well ahead and not done willy-nilly.
- Clear records of fishing effort, ie how long it took the angler to catch anything, are kept.
- Fishing methods are regulated and not just a free-for-all.
- The fish you catch show a good spread of sizes from babies through to leviathans; all one size is not necessarily a healthy sign.

QUOTE UNQUOTE

Fishing people are different. They are outdated and yet know exactly where they stand in the world.
Janna Bialek, American feminist writer

DRUNK GOLDFISH WINS REPRIEVE

In the spirit of tequila aficionados putting worms in their favourite drink, a Canadian bar momentarily started a new craze of goldfish shooters. Apparently customers were inspired by the cult TV series *Fear Factor* and fuelled by a surfeit of the hard stuff, decided to swallow the bar's pet goldfishes whole, having first anesthetised them in a shot glass of neat tequila or Jagermeister, a German liqueur. The fashion was short-lived however after the bar received a complaint from the Calgary Humane Society, which claimed cruelty to the fish. The bar was also then told by the city health inspectors to stop selling the novelty drink on the grounds that the fish may not be fit for human consumption, as they had not been inspected first prior to swallowing.

All this meant the goldfish won a reprieve from a last swim in tequila and instead met their maker as a meal for the pub's other piscatorial resident, the pet catfish. A double-edged sword perhaps?

CLOSED FOR BUSINESS

Most freshwater fish in the UK need a break away from anglers' attentions. This rest period or 'close season' is normally the allotted time that the fish have to spawn and continue the species, so by law, anglers must stop fishing and give them a break.

Here are some examples:

1. You cannot fish for coarse fish species between 15 March and 15 June.

2. You cannot fish for brown trout between 6 October and 15 March.

3. You cannot fish for salmon on the River Tweed between 30 November and 1 February.

4. You cannot fish for salmon on the River Tay between 15 October and 15 January.

5. You generally cannot fish for migratory fish (like salmon) in numerous other rivers around the UK, from mid October to early February. Check the exact local opening and closing times before you go, to avoid disappointment.

A LITERARY CATCH

We may say of angling as Dr Boteler said of strawberries: 'Doubtless God could have made a better berry, but doubtless God never did'; and so, (if I might be judge,) God never did make a more calm, quiet, innocent recreation than angling.

Izaak Walton, *The Compleat Angler.*

BRITAIN'S FISHING FASHIONS

Dapper Irish

While their fishing brothers across the Irish Sea pussyfooted around with delicately tied exact imitations of real flies, the Irish got straight to the point, saving a bundle on fur and feather and by sticking live insects (usually mayflies) on the hook. After all, why bother with fiddly dressings when there are so many natural bugs flying about? These 'baits' were and still are fished by a method known as dapping. This involves a huge rod of about 18 feet and a line of dapping floss with a smidgeon of nylon on the end, on to which you tie the hook and its wriggly occupants. No casting is involved, you simply hoick the rod up to the perpendicular and then let the wind blow the fly and line out so that it dips enticingly on the water. With any luck, a fish sees this bunch of insects bobbing about and comes up to nab them before they disappear again. Simple, but effective.

TEN USEFUL WEBSITES

www.hooklinks.net
Hours of fun surfing here as this site puts you in touch
with a zillion other fishy sites.

www.coarse-fisherman.co.uk
Everything from the carp/pike/perch enthusiast with knobs on.

www.sea-fishing.org
Salt water fishing, tackle, news, reviews etc.

www.fishandfly.co.uk
Probably the best long runner of the fly fishing websites in the UK.

www.content-angler.com
Quirky American site explaining the ephemeral joys of fishing.

www.flytyingforum.com
An absolute must for the avid fly-tyer, lots of
pics and how to tie them.

www.fishing-highland.co.uk
Excellent site for finding out more about fishing in the Scottish
highlands.

www.anglerscircle.co.uk
A chat site where you can engage in everything from fishy facts to
fishy gossip.

www.fishingworks.com
Comprehensive info site on everything from fishing guides, to travel
to hiring a boat.

www.fishing.co.uk
Fishing articles, holidays, book reviews... you name it, it's here.

SOLDIER PALMERS

The Soldier Palmer is a popular trout fly commonly used on many
Scottish and Irish loughs. Its history could effectively stretch back to
Roman times, when a Roman, Aelianus, wrote of fishing for trout
with an artificial fly. It had a red body and brown feather hackle,
designed in a very similar way to the later British version. Palmers
were probably the first type of very basic artificial fly used to catch
trout in Britain, as they are little more than a hook with a feather
twisted round it from end to end. Niceties like winged patterns did
not seem to appear until the fifteenth century. The name Soldier
Palmer appears to come from medieval times, when soldiers returning
from Holy Wars wearing the uniform of the bright red cross would
have (presumably brown-leaved) palms strewn at their feet.

ALL AT SEA

While sea fishing, you can employ any or all of the following:
Bullets • Legers • Jigs
Multipliers • Paternosters
Pendulums • Rigs • Shock leaders
Stop knots • Swivels

OPEN WIDE!

It's often said that *Esox lucius*, otherwise known as the pike, is the shark of the freshwater world. Certainly he's a greedy predator, eating everything and anything he can wrap his jaws around. Pike grow to huge sizes – specimens up to 19 kilos have been caught in Britain and there are probably larger ones lurking out there. The fish is instantly recognisable by its long greenish-gold body, topped off with a mighty mouth full of sharp incisors. These teeth face back towards the throat, making it extremely difficult for any prey (or your fingers) to be extracted from its grasp. Pike have been known to devour anything from rats and birds to water voles and trout; if they can fit it in their mouth, they will eat it. Tales abound of the pike's voracity. One of the best is from the *Fishing Gazette* written by H Band in 1883: 'A few paces below me I noticed three young sand martins perched on a bough, which overhung the water. They could hardly fly, and the old ones were fluttering about them. My float lay motionless on the surface. Suddenly there was a tremendous splash in the water directly down under the withie bough, which swung up and down. One bird was still on the bough, and another, after fluttering about a little, again settled down on it. I looked on in amazement; the waves, caused by the splash, spread over the river, the surface became smooth and still again, but one bird was missing.

'A bite at my line recalled my attention to fishing; but presently there was another splash under the bough, which swayed about again – the other bird was missing, and now only one remained, balancing itself with difficulty on the swinging branch. That the thief was a pike was quite evident. I stuck my rod-butt into the soft bank, and quietly approached the spot, soon finding a convenient place from which to reconnoitre. Steadily I watched for a long time. The final dash of the pike occurred so violently, so suddenly – and this time from the side where I had been sitting – that I could only get an instants view of what had happened. The third sand martin was gone. The swaying bough grew still again and all was over.'

---

36 Total *weight, in metric tonnes, of Scottish sea trout caught by all methods in 2002. Actual weight was 36.5 metric tonnes*

SIX GOOD REASONS TO EAT MORE FISH

1. Fish contain omega-3 oils, which are known to assist in the prevention of heart disease and strokes. Consumers who eat fish regularly ie at least twice a week, tend to have fewer heart attacks and strokes. All fish is good, however, providing they all come from a sustainable source, fresh tuna, herring, mackerel, mullet and salmon are all especially high in that magic ingredient omega-3.

2. Fish are low in the 'bad' saturated fats. The healthiest ways to cook your fish are by steaming, grilling or baking. Fish that is deep fried in thick batter (as most fish suppers are) is delicious but loses its important low-fat qualities. Pity.

3. Fish are good for your bones. Canned fish like sardine and salmon contain softened edible bones, which are said to add to your calcium levels. A glass of milk with a plate of steamed fresh fish might have a similar effect.

4. Fish is good for diabetes sufferers. Since those with diabetes are at greater risk from heart disease, a diet containing lots of fish will help lessen that risk.

5. Fish can aid in the treatment of asthmatics. Research suggests that children who eat fish regularly are less likely to develop asthma.

6. Fish are comparatively inexpensive. You can derive as much nutritional benefit from a fresh mackerel as you can from beef mince, with the added bonus you do not consume as much saturated fats.

QUOTE UNQUOTE

Truth is when one fisherman calls another fisherman a liar.
Anon

FAMOUS LADIES IN FISHING

Princess Grace of Monaco
In the 1950s and early 1960s, the late Princess Grace was a renowned angler and madly keen on coarse fishing. Her exploits were rarely recorded however, as she would fish incognito away from the prying paparazzi, disguised as an elderly stooped crone. Only a privileged few ever knew who it really was participating on the open match circuit, where she was highly adept at whizzing out a mean swim feeder and bagging double nets of 'dustbin lids' – large bream to you and me.

I did say, cast your net in the water...

A BIT FISHY

Yellow, white, grey, blue, black, red are all colours that can be used to describe which fish species? And which of these coloured fish contains some non-European genes?
Answer on page 153.

CATCHING THE COELACANTH

Unlike the Loch Ness monster whose presence has never advanced beyond the realms of myth and mystery, the coelacanth (pronounced 'sealakanth') has been caught and confirmed as one of the world's few remaining living fossils. Its origins have been traced back some 400 million years to a time when dinosaurs ruled the earth. With its limb-like fins and luminescent eyes, it is thought that the coelacanth was one of the first fish to crawl out of the sea and on to land. On becoming land-based, the species slowly evolved, first into reptiles, then mammals and finally, a long way down the ecological ladder, mankind itself. Led by the ever-enthusiastic JLB Smith, an ichthyologist version of Indiana Jones, the modern story of the finding of the coelacanth began in 1938 and was not finally unravelled until 1998. It was a drama-filled trail of research across continents, over and under seas and through many miles of red tape. You can read more in *A Fish Caught in Time* by Samantha Weinberg.

A LITERARY CATCH

ANGLING, is an art which, as it pleads great antiquity, so the knowledge thereof is with much difficulty to be obtained; but some observations concerning it will not be amiss. And first, the angler must remember, by no means to fish in light and dazzling apparel, but his clothing must be of a dark sky colour; and at the places where he uses to angle he should once in four or five days cast in corn boiled soft; if for carp or tench oftener: he may also cast in garbage, beasts livers, worms chopped in pieces or grains steeped in blood and dried, which will attract the fish thither.

Henry James, *Sportmans Dictionary*

KIDS ALL-AMERICAN FISHING DERBY

According to the www.fish4fun.com website, if a company sponsors youth fishing, it endears the company products to the kids and their parents. This philosophy seems to have worked; the original sponsors were Wal-Mart, but since they set the standard, a whole bunch of companies have jumped on the sponsor bandwagon. These include, in no particular order:

Kraft Foods
Edy's Grand Ice Cream
Repel Insect Repellent
Purell Instant Hand Sanitizer
DMF Bait Co
Nestle Waters North America
Bar-S Foods Co
Dubble Bubble Bubble Gum
EverStart Batteries
Band-Aid Adhesive Bandages

Which says quite a bit about kids and fishing expeditions...

FINDING THE GARDEN FLY

The 'garden fly' is a coy way of describing the earthworm, an excellent bait for stubborn, sulking fish. To extract worms quickly from unlikely looking soil – for example, a garden lawn – pour slightly warm, but not hot soapy water (water for the dishes containing a dose of washing up liquid is best) over a reasonable area and wait for about three to five minutes. The worms will magically appear at the surface and it is an easy exercise to pick them off and store them in a plastic container, with some fresh moss ready for use. It seems that the earthworm has a strong dislike for soap and comes up to the surface to escape it. Just don't tell everyone who told you this tip!

R Macdonald Robertson

Robertson did most of his fishing in Scotland in the 1920s and 1930s. He published three books on Scottish angling adventures between 1935 and 1948. His expansive tales of trout fishing derring-do, laced with a peculiar mix of folklore and fact, are eloquently set amongst lonely moors, racing rivers and stormy lochs. Robertson recalls fishing in a different era, a gentler time when it took days rather than hours to travel the length of Scotland. He is best known for his rollicking tale of the *Muckle Troot O'Dulnain* and for posting his catch south on the train, wrapped in cabbage leaves and sewn into a canvas bag. Although his writings are not much in vogue now, they still stand as enlightening and inspirational reads when compared with much of today's techno-obsessed scribblings.

QUOTE UNQUOTE

How far an angler can stretch the truth depends on how far he can stretch his arms.
Anon

PURISM

In the nineteenth century, angling purism was the height of dandified fashion. Then, if you described an angler as a purist, it meant he would only use an exquisitely-made dry fly to catch trout in a river and turn his nose firmly up at any other method. Not only that, but he would only cast the fly upstream and at a rising (actively feeding) trout. If fish were rising downstream or feeding below the surface, in which case a wet fly might catch it, tough, purists fished only the 'dray flay' upstream. Legendary nineteenth-century angler FM Halford can be credited for playing a significant part introducing the dry fly to a much wider audience of anglers; how-ever he did not quite anticipate how his followers would zeal-ously interpret his ideas. What for him began as a novel way of attracting trout on chalk-streams, rapidly turned into a society doctrine practised by those who saw themselves as the angling upper classes with their ideals firmly hooked into dogma. Even Halford as the 'Father of dry fly' began to despair at the behaviour of some of his cult followers declaring: 'Although respecting their scru-ples, this is in my humble opin-ion, riding the hobby to death'.

Thankfully the cult of purism has evolved into a more flexible approach and today old preju-dices are now all but buried.

PASS THE PROP

Fishing on Australia Day in 2003, an Australian trawler netted the catch of the year when it connected with a huge propeller from a 1940s naval plane. Fishing in their usual spot 14 miles off Ulladulla, the crew of the Arakiwa were astonished when, instead of hauling in a grand weighty catch of fish, an old propeller came to the surface. Although badly rusted, the propeller still had its five blades attached and the curling at the wing tips showed the force at which the original plane hit the water. The catch proved a costly exercise. It took the trawler a full four hours to get back to port, the tangled net cost AUS$8,000 to replace and the crew had to pay to hire a crane to get their unexpected catch out of the water.

A PIECE OF THE STREAM

Going fishing in the British Isles is still a relatively uncomplicated business; however, if the river, reservoir, lake or loch needs some form of attention there is always a bundle of red tape to get through. Here are a few of the bodies who are in some way involved with our water:

Department of Environment, Farming and Rural Affairs (DEFRA)
Environmental Agency England and Wales (EA)
English Nature
Fishing clubs
Local water authorities
Riparian Owners and lessees
Rivers Agency
Scottish Water
Scottish Fisheries Trusts
Scottish Salmon River Boards
Scottish Environmental Protection Agency (SEPA)
Scottish Natural Heritage (SNH)
World Wide Fund for Nature (WWF)

MUDDLING ALONG

The ancient art of muddling is a quaint way of attracting that small but precious English fish, the gudgeon. To be executed successfully, the angler needs to acquire a newly-cut sod of earth and, thus armed, wade into the river, place the sod in a fast-flowing bit of the current and then wait a while. This ploy will send out a cloud of silty earth into the current and is said to attract gudgeon from far and wide. The angler can then catch the fish at leisure. It is thought that muddling may be the origin of the modern word muddle, for certainly the modern word means a clouded view.

Minimum legal length, in centimetres, of a sea bass caught on the UK shoreline, 41
as recorded in the book Freshwater Fishes in Britain

FAMOUS GAME FISHING VENUES
AROUND THE UK

Across Britain there are fisheries with long-established and well-deserved reputations. These are a few of the best known:

In England	In Ireland
River Test	Lough Corrib
River Itchen	Lough Melvin
Blagdon Lake	Loch Erne
Chew Reservoir	Lough Conn
Rutland Reservoir	Lough Mask
Bewl Reservoir	Foyle Fishery
River Wharfe	Burishoole Fishery
River Teviot	Delphi Fishery

In Scotland	In Wales
River Tweed	River Towy
River Spey	River Teifi
River Tay	River Nevern
River Dee	Llyn Brenig
River Don	Talyllyn
Loch Leven	Lake Vyrnwy
Loch Watten	
Lake of Menteith	

BEFORE NYLON WAS INVENTED

In order to keep the fish from seeing and being spooked by the thick part of the fishing line, some form of tapered leader (the bit that joins hook to line) had to be made onto which would be attached the hook or fly. Fishing lines dating from the 1400s had their own in-built leader and were made from braided horsehair tapered down to a fine semi-invisible single strand of hair at the end of which would be the hook. These were neat and beautifully-made contraptions, but required careful attention otherwise they would snap. During the nineteenth century the old horsehair lines were replaced by silk lines, and then gut, which would be tied on at the end of the line to form the leader. The first gut was made from the entrails of a silkworm and later, until silk became scarcer, and then sheep's intestines provided a cheaper alternative. Whatever the type of gut, it still needed a huge amount of care. It had to be kept damp in order to avoid brittleness. All in all, anglers breathed a collective sigh of relief when the nylon leader was invented in the 1930s, and have never looked back.

KELLY'S EMERGENCY TROUT

The Kelly Kettle is familiar to anglers wanting a brew up on the river or lake. It's basically a fast-boiling water pot shaped rather like a milk churn; all you need is a small fire or primus for heat, and tea will be served within minutes. However, if you are feeling hungry after catching a few trout but are reluctant to leave the water, the Kelly will come to your rescue, for it will double admirably as a cooking pot.

To do justice to the delicious vaguely sweet flesh of a super-fresh trout caught by your own hand, gut and remove the innards and season the cavity with sea salt and a little white pepper. Remove the head and score the sides with a sharp knife to allow juice absorption. Stuff the trout with a glob of butter, some herbs – fresh tarragon and parsley preferably – and wrap tightly in tin foil. Place the package into the Kelly and heat gently for about 10 minutes or so. Remove and decant into whatever serving dish you have with you and garnish with more parsley and slices of lemon. This goes well with a gentle mustard sauce, green salad and minted potatoes, but if you can't bring the whole shebang with you, just eat the trout with your fingers straight from the tin foil. Finally, remember to wash out the kettle well afterwards.

QUOTE UNQUOTE

You say well, where are the fish, ha, ha, they say look, bub, can't you get it through your thick skull there is more to fishing than catching fish.
Ed Zern, American writer and angler

SUPERSTITIONS OF THE SEAFARERS

Blood and guts

Sailors are notoriously superstitious. When going fishing off the north east coast of Scotland, the men of Morayshire regarded it as unlucky to begin the season before blood had been shed. Wishing any seaman 'Have a good trip' was desperately unlucky if he had not seen blood spilt before you gave him your best. Often fist-fights would be started in order to render this fresh blood. Fishermen of Portlessie, in north east Scotland would punch the nose of anyone silly enough to wish them 'bon voyage', thus dispelling lurking demons by immediately drawing blood. Onboard boat it was apparently also considered bad luck not to 'take blood' from the first fish to come up over the side. What the sailors did with the blood is anyone's guess.

HOW FISH GOT THEIR NAMES

Char

Artic char (or charr) are a beautifully-coloured native fish featuring in deep lochs and lakes in the north of Scotland, parts of Wales and in Ireland. The fish derive their name from ancient Gaelic which denoted the fish as 'tarr-dhearg' or 'tar deargan' or even 'tarragan'. All of these spellings meant 'red bellies' or 'red fellows'. Over time the Gaelic name became corrupted into English first to char and then to charr. The English often recorded old Scots words phonetically rather than observe their true spellings. Often they would stick a double 'r' on a Scots word for emphasis or perhaps to cover up the fact they could not quite get their teeth round the soft Gaelic pronunciation of 'tar', which sounds like t-haar.

NICKNAMES FOR FISH

Barse – perch
Coley – saithe
Cuddies – saithe
Cuddy – freshwater Artic char
Culle – bullhead
Finnock – young immature sea trout
Fluke – flounder
Haddies – haddock
Jack barrel – minnow
Kipper – dark red coloured salmon ready to spawn
Pope – ruffe
Sellacks – young cod or saithe
Silver darlings – herring
Tiddlebat – three-spined stickleback

A LITERARY CATCH

The old Scandinavian writers attribute to the sea-serpent a length of six hundred feet, with a head closely resembling that of a horse, black eyes, and a kind of white mane. According to them, it is only met with in the ocean, where it suddenly rears itself up like a mast of a ship of the line, and gives vent to hissing noises which appal the hearer, like a tempest roar. The Norwegian poets compare its progress to the flight of a swift arrow. When the fishermen descry it they row in the direction of the sun, the monster being unable to see when its head is turned towards the planet. They say that it revolves sometimes in a circle around the doomed vessel, whose crew thus find themselves assailed on every side.

The Mysteries of the Ocean by Mangin,
a nineteenth-century French writer

---

44 *Cost, in pounds sterling, of a week's fishing with four-fish-limit per day, on Wales's Llandegfedd Reservoir in 2005*

A fish from the river, a wand from the wood and a deer from the forest – three thefts no Gael is ashamed of at any time.

Anon

A BIT OF WIND

When fishing for an easily spooked fish like a trout or a salmon you need a bit of wind to disguise your intentions. However the wind has to be 'right' – most of the time experienced anglers will tell you it's most definitely not! Here are a few examples of winds good and bad:

Cats' paws – A frightful wind that is so fierce it breaks the water into scuds, which then chase each other over the lake. From a distance this looks like cats' paws dancing over the water. On seeing this, seasoned anglers will usually retire to the nearest hostelry.

Gales – English gales and Scottish gales are not the same. In England anything over 10 knots is a gale; in northern Scotland it has to be over 25 knots before the wind becomes a gale and disrupts the day.

A good wave – This refers to waves on a large lake or loch. A good wave causes the boat to drift along at a steady pace and allows you to fish with disguise but without discomfort.

A dapping wind – There is a special type of fishing known as dapping. It is seen mainly on Irish loughs and a dapping wind allows the unique light floss line to billow forth in front of the boat.

A flat calm – For fly fishers this effect can be an absolute pain. A flat calm means nothing to hide deadly intentions, and unless the fisher is very deft in his casting technique, fish are liable to keep their heads down. The fishing then assumes the mantle of what is politely known as 'very difficult'.

West winds – a west wind is normally a warm wet one, good for well-kitted out anglers and good for fish, as it encourages them to feed. Fishy folklore has it that a west wind falls away in the evening and that just before darkness fish feed frenetically and the angler has a good chance of bagging a few. Similar things are said about warm winds from the south, which apparently 'blow the fly into the fish's mouth'.

East/North winds – probably the least favoured winds as they are usually cold and sharp and are generally thought to make the fish less active. Not always entirely accurate, however, as the fish have a pretty uniform environment underwater. Anglers tend to get chilled and miserable way before the fish does.

BE KIND TO YOUR CATCH

In coarse fishing the (largely inedible) catch is almost always released after being weighed and photographed. In sea fishing some fish are put back after recording their size, while some good eating species like cod or mackerel are kept. Game fishing is different. Some fisheries operate a 'catch and release' rule, usually in the name of conservation of particular endangered species like Atlantic salmon. This means fish have to be returned alive and kicking. Here's how to be kind to your catch:

1. Use a knotless net which does not rub the delicate protective mucous of the back of the fish.
2. Use a rod and line fit for the job. Avoid playing heavy fish to a standstill on flimsy tackle.
3. Wet your hands before handling the fish.
4. If you want a photograph, keep the fish in the landing net in the water, lift from there, quick snap and back she goes into the net and from there into the stream.
5. Keep all fish out of the water for as short a time as possible.
6. When releasing a big fish, face it head on into the current, hold gently by the tail and allow the fish to get its gills going before letting it go. The days of 'throw it back' are long gone.
7. Similarly in lake fishing, hold the fish under the water by the tail and work it gently back and forth until it kicks and scoots off.
8. Using a barbless hook is sometimes compulsory. This allows the fish to be slipped off easily from the hook.

NOSING AROUND

It is said that fish are repelled by certain scents, yet attracted by others. Apparently fish exit stage left when they scent sun block, tobacco or insect repellent in the water. This happens quite frequently as anglers often forget to remove such pongs from their fingers before they tie on the fly. Scientists declare that fish find these strong smells pretty unattractive; however, the opposite is supposed to occur if a women ties on the fly. Salmon are said to be particularly attracted to a woman's scent. But it's not her Chanel No 5 that provides the attraction; it's her pheromones. Male salmon are said to make a beeline toward a woman's hormone-laden fly and ignore ones presented by men. Female pheromones apparently transfer on to the fly when a woman ties it on to the line, causing an insatiable response in the male fish population. The number of men using this as a feeble excuse when they fail to catch as many fish as the women has never been fully ascertained.

A LITERARY CATCH

All in a hot and copper sky
The bloody sun at noon
Right up above the mast did stand
No bigger than the Moon

Day after day, day after day
We struck, nor breath nor motion
As idle as a painted ship
Upon a painted ocean

Water, water every where
And all the boards did shrink
Water, water everywhere
Nor any drop to drink

The very deep did rot: O Christ!
That ever this should be!
Yea, slimy things did crawl with legs
Upon the slimy sea

Samuel Taylor Coleridge,
The Rime of the Ancient Marine

QUOTE UNQUOTE

Doing? What am I doing? Man, I am an angler!
Thomas Stoddart, nineteenth-century Scots angler

FISH TO CATCH FISH

In the sea virtually all fish will eat other fish, and a considerable number of species can be caught by using smaller fish as bait. Probably the best-known type of fish for this ploy is the mackerel, which, with its pungent oily smell and durability when cut in strips, makes it an ideal bait for pollack, saithe, dogfish and conger eel. Freshwater anglers in the Northern isles use strips of mackerel to tempt sea trout in brackish water. This they use on fly rod and floating line, casting the bait forward with a roll cast and then drawing the silvery slice quickly back towards them as if it were a small fleeing fish. Sand eel, whitebait, herring and squid are also used as bait cut to appropriate sizes and carefully threaded on hooks to avoid being lost. These baits are more often used on a spinning rod with multiplier reel rather than a fly rod.

TO MAKE A BOILIE

According to the website www.coarse-fisherman.co.uk, the best boilie (bait) recipe to attract big carp is as follows:

Ingredients
250g base mix
250g ultra-mix
6 medium eggs
Colouring
5ml maple syrup
1 tsp boilie sweetener

Recipe
1. Mix the base mix and the ultra-mix together until thoroughly blended.
2. Form a well in the mix and add in the eggs.
3. Add the colouring and flavouring.
4. Add the sweetener and mix thoroughly.
5. Spread some of the mixture (half at a time) on the table and roll into a sausage shape.
6. Cut into small cubes and roll into balls.
7. Place the 'boilies' into a pan of boiling water and boil for 30 seconds, to one minute.
8. Remove from the water and drain on a tea towel til cool.
9. Place boilies in a plastic bag and dispel the air.

A BIT FISHY

Where would you find a *Cristivomer namaycush*
(and no, this is not an anagram)?
Answer on page 153.

MACNABBING

A 'Macnab' is a highland sporting challenge of shooting a grouse, catching a salmon and killing a stag all in the one day. The custom is believed to have begun after John Buchan wrote his classic novel *John Macnab*. While in the early 1900s a Macnab was relatively easy to achieve, today's scarcity of wild game makes the challenge an almost impossible one, with a considerable modicum of luck involved. Frequently, sportsmen will have little difficulty nabbing the stag and the grouse but have their ambitions confounded by the lack of Atlantic salmon in Scotland rivers. Either that or they will hook a fish first thing, shoot the stag and then find the grouse have all shown a clean pair of heels and winged it over on to a neighbouring inaccessible moor.

Cutting across another angler's drift is not always a good idea.

TO RUSSIA WITH LOVE

Match fishing, which is angling for coarse fish on a competitive basis, is a hugely expensive game. Amongst other paraphernalia, you need: umbrellas, a seat, sometimes a tent, camping gear, wet weather gear, rods, poles and reels, rod rests, fish bite alarms, floats, swim feeders, keep net, landing net, hooks, weights and a zillion different baits all in separate boxes. By the time you've lugged all this down to the river it might be time for a lie down, never mind start fishing. And then there is the touchy problem of security. Leaving your tackle unguarded can result in theft or sabotage or both, and it is apparently a major headache for match fishermen and it's a particular problem if you're fishing with less well-equipped competitors. The England match fishing team 'Drennan England' were concerned about exactly this when they faced the prospect of attending the 2005 men's world championships in Russia, a dangerous place to fish at the best of times. They were so worried that expensive kit might disappear en route or at the cross border checkpoints that the deputy mayor of Moscow had to give his personal assurance that the equipment would be safe before Drennan England were prepared to jet off to Russia's rivers and lakes.

FISH WARS

Icelandic cod wars

The cold waters around Iceland are rich in fish, particularly cod, a fish that forms the staple ingredient of that beloved British dish, the fish supper. Back in 1958 the Icelanders declared a 12-mile limit around their home shores and excluded other foreign trawlers from fishing there. Britain responded that this rule broke international maritime law and infringed the 'freedom of the seas'. Cod, said the government, would be fished for off Iceland, as it had always been.

After this announcement feelings ran high. The British Embassy in Reykjavik was stoned and tense scuffles and stand-offs between Icelandic patrols and British frigates became a common occurrence. In 1961 the conflict was resolved, only to start up again in the early 1970s when Iceland moved the goalposts again, pushing out the limit first to 50 miles then 200 miles. More tetchy quarrels resulted at sea until the Brits finally and somewhat reluctantly agreed to annual catches and conservation areas.

FAMOUS ANGLERS AND THEIR DAY JOBS

Ian Botham – *Retired cricketer*
Bernard Cribbens – *Actor*
Nick Faldo – *Golfer*
Sir Max Hastings – *Former editor of the* Daily Telegraph
George Melley – *Jazz musician*
Jeremy Paxman – Newsnight *presenter*
Chris Tarrant – *Presenter of* Who Wants to be a Millionaire
Paul Whitehouse – *Actor famed for one half of Smashie and Nicey*
Paul Young – *Scottish actor*

TIGHT LINES ON THE THAMES

In Spring 2005 a new angling project called 'Tightlines' was launched on London's rambling network of canals. The project, funded by the Environment Agency and operated by the environmental charity Thames21, will work towards introducing a range of fishing skills to both young and old (age is no barrier apparently), while fostering a wider respect for London's unique waterside environment. Thames21 will not only provide the instructors and the essential gear to learn to fish, but also will be encouraging water users to be more environmentally aware and act responsibly to create clean, safe and sustainable waterways for everyone to enjoy. Laudable aims indeed.

A LITERARY CATCH

Three fishers went sailing away to the west,
Away to the west as the sun went down;
Each thought on the woman who loved him the best,
And the children stood watching them out of the town;
For men must work, and women must weep,
Though the harbour bar be moaning.

Three wives sat up in the lighthouse tower,
And they trimmed the lamps as the sun went down;
They looked at the squall, and they looked at the shower,
And the night-rack came rolling up ragged and brown.
But men must work, and women must weep,
Though storms be sudden, and waters deep,
And the harbour bar be moaning.

Three corpses lay out on the shining sands
In the morning gleam as the tide went down,
And the women are weeping and wringing their hands
For those who will never come home to the town;
For men must work, and women must weep,
And the sooner it's over, the sooner to sleep;
And good-bye to the bar and its moaning.

Charles Kingsley,
The Three Fishers

TRADING PLAICES

In 2005 according to a report in *The Times*, fish have become a global commodity to be wheeled and dealed in, rather like oil or gold. Gone for ever are the days when consumers contented themselves with Friday's little bit of haddock or cod. Today's customers want tuna, grouper, sea bream, snapper or swordfish, and that's just for starters. Demand for exotic seafood has also now reached an all-time high and sea fishermen have had to go hi-tech to keep up with this leap in demand. According to *The Times* report, fishermen have live web cams or use mobile phone photography at sea to take pictures of their most recent catches, then send the pictures by email to waiting fish dealers who bid online for the fish. Effectively this means a fish caught in the Indian Ocean can be bought at sea, landed, processed by the fish buyer, shipped on ice by plane, zoomed to Billingsgate market, resold through your local fish shop and cooked to perfection by your fair hand, all in the space of two days. Phew!

In 1658 Richard Franck wrote *Northern Memoirs*, which was finally published in 1694 when the publisher had collected enough ink. The full title runs as follows:

*Northern Memoirs
Calculated for the
Meridian of Scotland*

*Wherein most of the Cities, Citadels,
Sea Ports, Castles, Forts, Fortresses
Rivers, and Rivulets, are compendiously
described*

*Together with choice Collections of various Discoveries,
Remarkable Observations, Theological
Notions, Political Axioms, National Intrigues,
Polemick Inferences, Contemplations, Speculations,
and several curious and industrious Inspections,
lineally drawn from Antiquaries, and
other noted and intelligible Persons of Honour
and Eminency*

To which is added:

*The Contemplative and Practical Angler
By way of a diversion. With a Narrative of that dextrous
and mysterious Art experimented in England, and perfected
in more remote and solitary Parts of Scotland.
By way of Dialogue.*

It was not a best seller.

FLIES WITH INNUENDO

Flying Cs

The first thing that most of the non-angling fraternity ask about the flying C is what the 'C' stands for. Believe it or not, the angler who tied this fly had made the body of it with a condom, hopefully unused. In order not to offend other fellow angler's delicate sensibilities, he named the finished creation the flying C. It seems the latex material of the condom is particularly good at keeping the shape of the fly and as it wiggles slightly in the water, fish are greatly attracted to it. Flying Cs have been remarkably successful at catching salmon in the UK and have given new meaning to the phrase 'protected species'.

A BIT FISHY

To what fish do these names relate?
coles, grays, coomasaham, trevelyans, blunt nosed and scharffs.
Answer on page 153.

HERRINGS RED OR OTHERWISE

To explain the meaning of the saying 'a red herring' is not quite as easy as one might imagine. Back in the eighteenth century the herring could indeed be red, but it did not come fresh from the sea like that. It seems that newly-caught silvery herrings had the alarming habit of going off extremely quickly. In order to preserve the catch a combination of methods could be used, all of which involved a degree of salting and smoking. Different herring ports developed different recipes for the preserving process; for example, Yarmouth had its 'bloater', while Arbroath had its 'kipper' or 'smokie'. Further afield the Germans developed the 'buckling', a rather similar process to the bloater. However the oldest and most famous preserved fish was the 'red herring', which, after lashings of smoking and salting over perhaps two days, did indeed come out a brownish-red.

Nowadays, according to EU regulations, the salt content and carcinogenic qualities of the old red herrings alone might make them impossible to sell; however, the name still lives on albeit under a different guise. Today if we say something is a red herring it means a devious point has been thrown into the argument in order to mislead us. According to *Brewer's Dictionary*, this term is derived from the practise of trailing a (very smelly) red herring across – or more likely around – a field in order to put hunting dogs off the scent of a real fox. Apparently, farmers dismayed at hunters charging through their valuable crops in pursuit of a fox sometimes laid false scents (presumably away from their crops) in order to stop the hounds and huntsmen in their tracks.

The story does not end there, however, for in a typically odd twist, eighteenth-century books on methods of fox hunting do not make any mention of using fish to distract the hounds. In fact in Cox's *Gentlemen's Recreations* circa 1686, a red herring is mentioned as helping to train dogs to follow scent, not put them off it. Cox relates the trailing of a dead fox, cat or in case of necessity a red herring over three or four miles and then 'laying the dogs on the scent'. How the red herring was then converted to a spurious distraction seems never to be properly explained, but then that's red herrings for you.

Too many rods spoil the loch.

I SPY

You might at first be at a loss to see the connection between a World War Two subterfuge aid and a device employed in the gentle art of trout fishing. It seems that British and American agents employed silent one-man floatation devices to creep out and spy on and/or sabotage enemy ships. These floats were rather like large rubber rings complete with an interior canvas seat. The agent would don fins and a wet suit, sit in the middle of the ring, put any gear he needed to keep dry on its raised surface or 'apron' and then paddle quietly out on the water toward the enemy. In the 1980s American manufacturers revived the idea, only this time the angler was the hunter and the quarry a wary trout. Anglers using these devices called float tubes, U-boats or belly boats, look rather akin to a very large duck. Fashion accessories they ain't, but float tubes remain a practical silent mode of water transport, avoiding the need for hiring boats and outboards while allowing the angler to creep up on the unsuspecting fish.

WHAT ANGLERS SUFFER IN THE NAME OF THEIR SPORT

Tangle-itus

This illness will almost invariably strike any type of angler who has just spotted the fish of a lifetime. Unfortunately, instead of casting out a delicate line to the waiting leviathan, the fisher launches out little more than a ball of knitting, and then spends the next half an hour trying to untangle it. Of course by the time all is unpicked and well again, the fish has made for cover, if not completely disappeared.

WHICH FLY?

The range of fishing flies on the market today is quite extraordinary. What began as but a twist of fur and feather now encompasses a cast of thousands. Here are just a few:

Blobs • Bubbled sedges • Buzzers
CDC flies • Coneheads • Czech mates
Daddies • Damsels • Depth charge nymphs
Diawl bach's • Dog nobblers • Dry flies
Emergers • General purpose nymphs
Hackled wets • Hoppers • Krystal eggs
Magic circle nymphs • Mayflies
Minky boobies • Muddlers • Parachute flies
Pheasant tails • Tadpoles • Thorax flies
Traditional wets • Zonkers

QUOTE UNQUOTE

*Gudgeon-fishing!... I maintain to be, par excellence, the
sport of the poet and the philosopher.*
H Cholmondeley Pennel, nineteenth-century English angling author

FISHING FOR MARK TWAIN

According to the Missouri State Parks Department, ice fishing in the depths of winter on the 18,000-acre Mark Twain Lake is not advised due to fluctuating water levels, as well as variable ice thickness. However, when the lake is not frozen, visiting anglers can enjoy fishing for a wide variety of fish including largemouth bass, carp, bluegill, walleye, catfish and the delightfully named crappie. If you don't come prepared with your own boat for the Mark Twain water, you can conveniently move over to the Tom Sawyer Lake for some bank fishing. There is no mention of the 'Huckleberry Finn River' being available yet, but they're working on it.

TEN MOST INFLUENTIAL FIGURES IN BRITISH FLY FISHING

All of these anglers have helped to shape British freshwater fishing into what we know today:

Dame Juliana Berners – Fifteenth-century sporting nun and editor of the *The Treatise of Fishing with an Angle*, the first fisherman's 'Bible'.

Isaak Walton – Seventeenth-century angler and author of the first edition of the ground breaking *Compleat Angler*.

Charles Cotton – Seventeenth century angler and contributor of skills to the expanded second edition of the *The Compleat Angler*.

Col R Venables – Seventeenth century angler, way ahead of his time recording angling skills which were forgotten, and then reborn in the nineteenth century.

T Stoddart – Nineteenth-century Scottish angler who opened up Scottish angling to the wider view.

WC Stewart – Nineteenth-century Scottish angler who fundamentally changed river fly fishing forever, by introducing upstream casting with a wet fly.

William Scrope – Nineteenth-century salmon angler who laid down the foundations of the salmon fly and how to fish it.

FM Halford – Nineteenth- and early twentieth-century angler acknowledged as the principal promoter of the art of dry fly fishing in the UK. His attention to detail made his fly tying skills unsurpassable for many years.

GM Skues – Nineteenth- and early twentieth-century angler. The doyen of a style of fishing known as the 'upstream nymph', he introduced new skills to the wider angling public.

Hugh Falkus – Twentieth-century angler who by his writing and broadcasting made game fishing seem much more understandable and therefore accessible.

FAMOUS LADIES IN FISHING

Muriel Constance Foster

The little diary *Days on Sea Loch and River* written and illustrated by Muriel Foster, stands as testimony to angling from another, altogether more genteel, time. Muriel's superb watercolour drawings (she studied at the Slade School of Art) bring life to her meticulous handwritten recording of fishy successes and failures and the wonderful mannerly asides like 'Weather altogether beastly', make for wonderfully unique reading.

ONE OF A KIND

The famous River Tweed is unique in several respects:

1. It is the only river in the UK to rise in Scotland, near Moffat, but reach the sea in England at Berwick on Tweed.
2. It is the only river in Scotland to have unique fishing legislation relating solely to its waters.
3. It's also the only river in Scotland that has a statute declaring the care of all fish within the river system, including trout and grayling and not just the more lucrative salmon.
4. It's the only river in Europe where the trout have a 20% salmon gene, which means they have behavioural characteristics more like salmon than trout.
5. The Tweed is the only river in the UK that has 'commissioners' who look after the conservation and general management of the stream.

A LITERARY CATCH

A rod twelve feet long and a ring of wire, A winder and barrel, will help thy desire In killing a Pike; but the forked stick, With a slit and a bladder, – and that other fine trick, Which our artists call snap, with a goose or a duck, – Will kill two for one, if you have any luck; The gentry of Shropshire do merrily smile, To see a goose and a belt of fish beguile; When a Pike suns himslefe and a-frogging doth go, The two-inched hook is better, I know, Than the ord'nary snaring: but still I must cry, When The Pike is at home, minde the cookery.

Thomas Barker, *The Art of Angling*

ONE FOR THE POT

Sporting estates flourished during the nineteenth century, reaching their heyday prior to World War One. Rivers rich in salmon became not only the playground of the aristocracy, but also the haunt of the itinerant poacher. While the old crafty local angler taking a fish home 'for the pot' was by and large tolerated, commercially-orientated poaching gangs, often based in towns and cities, grew greatly in number. These gangs of 'heavies' would travel to the country, armed with anything from a gun to a baseball bat, and would extract as many fish as possible and then return to the city to sell their spoils. Their often violent presence on British salmon rivers continued for at least 150 years and only lessened when the severe decline of the Atlantic salmon made much of their activities unviable.

HOW FISH GOT THEIR NAMES

Trout

The earliest reference to trout occurs in eleventh-century English literature where trout at that time were called 'sceote' or 'sceotan'. Sceotan seems to be Old English meaning to rush, dart or shoot and obviously describes more the movement of the fish in water, rather than its fishing qualities. After the Normans arrived the sceote name for this fish changed first to 'truht' (Norman French), which then later became trout. By the time Dame Juliana edited the ground breaking *The Treatise of Fishing with an Angle* in 1496, the word trout was firmly established and the Dame enthusiastically describes the trout as 'a ryght feruente byter', literally 'a frequent biter', meaning an excellent sporting fish willing to come to the anglers fly or bait.

SHARKS AIN'T FUSSY

According to VM Coppleson who wrote *Shark Attack* in 1959, the following diverse items have been found in sharks' stomachs:

Three overcoats
One fully grown spaniel with collar
Several legs of mutton
Large piece of sacking
Head and forelegs of a bulldog
One nylon raincoat
One porpoise skull
Half a ham
Numerous sea birds
Numerous fish
Hind quarter of a pig
Assorted porcupine spines
Several lumps of horse flesh
One driving licence

A LITERARY CATCH

I am not a good fisherman myself, I devoted a considerable amount of attention to the subject at one time, and was getting on, as I thought fairly well; but the old hands told me that I should never be any real good at it, and advised me to give it up. They said that I was an extremely neat thrower, and that I seemed to have plenty of gumption for the thing, and quite enough constitutional laziness. But they were quite sure I should never make anything of a fisherman. I had not got sufficient imagination.

Jerome K Jerome, *Three Men in a Boat*

Length, in centimetres, of a spurdog that can be legally caught off the shoreline or in a boat in UK (sea) waters

A NORMAN INVASION

It is likely that the very first anglers in Britain came from Western Europe, probably during the Norman Invasion. The Normans arrived bearing not only arms but also fishing rods, which the English later deemed to call in their uniquely convoluted way 'angles'. Actually the word 'angle' originally referred to the bend in a fishing hook, somehow it got transferred to the rod and then finally to the man using it. Hence anything loosely to do with fishing became known as 'angling'. The first fishing rods were little more than long poles, and reels did not come into use until the 1600s. It is not thought the Normans invented rod fishing *per se*, but they may have procured the idea from Mediterranean countries where the 'Bolognese' rod was and still is, in common use. These rods, up to 20 foot or so, were the most basic of bait rods; all the angler needed to do was extend the rod over the water and dangle in the line and baited hook in the hope of attracting dinner. Seems the Normans not only created war widows but also fishing widows. They have a lot more to answer for than you might think!

QUOTE UNQUOTE

Fly fishing is a way of hooking into the world, being part of the swirling current and the riffle patterns on a river.
Ailm Travler, twentieth-century American author, angler and poet

THE WORLD'S MOST CAUGHT FISH AND WHO EATS THEM

Peruvian anchovy – 7.2 million tonnes of this prolific little fish, also known as the Peruvian anchoveta, were landed in 2001. Mainly caught in subtropical waters where it swims in massive shoals and feeds mainly on plankton. With this tonnage, that's a heck of a lot of pizza garnish.

Walleye pollack – Found in Alaskan waters, this is a long-living hardy fish surviving up to 15 years in its native waters if not harvested first. Around 3.1 million tonnes of this fish were caught by commercial netsmen in 2001 with a lot of the catch exported to the Japanese and Chinese sector.

Chilean jack mackerel – If you buy tinned mackerel in the UK with or without an accompanying sticky sauce, the chances are you will be eating this fish. About 2.5 million tonnes of the little critters were harvested from the south Pacific where they feed harmlessly on small shellfish and fish larvae.

Not quite a mermaid but...

SPARE THE ROD

According to James Leighton Hardy in the book *The House the Hardy Brothers Built*, the illustrious 'House of Hardy' fishing rod manufacturers treated the arrival of fibreglass as a rod-making material in the 1950s, with the deepest of suspicion. They feared rods made of this new material might put their bamboo rods out of business. So much so that they even conspired to make some poor-quality fibreglass rods in an attempt to convince the public that fibreglass would never catch on and that Hardy's cane rods were still the essential piece of kit.

Their subterfuge failed and fibreglass rods became the new surefire winner from the 1950s to around the mid 1970s, when carbon fibre took over as the new rod material.

THE GILLIE'S REVENGE

The gillie (a Scottish term meaning young boy and/or helper) will act as a guide to the salmon fisher on a river. He can quite literally make or break the day. Gillies are known for their deep abiding love, not only of fishing but also of whisky. Should their charge fail to regularly produce a surfeit of the latter, gillies have been known to extract revenge by the following means:

1. Fail to tell the guest his fly was cracked off on a stone behind at least half an hour ago, and leave him thrashing away with a long piece of nylon and no chance of hooking anything.

2. Give the myopic guest a casting stance on a flat stone covered in a thin layer of slippery algae and then tell him to cast vigorously.

3. Turn the boat into the wind and gun the engine hard while the guest is still trying to don his waterproof.

4. Put his charge on a river pool with a surfeit of undergrowth and point out the best salmon lies happen to be with gorse bushes in front and leafy alder trees directly behind.

A LITERARY CATCH

Fishing, if a fisher may protest,
Of pleasures is the sweet'st of sports the best,
Of exercises the most excellent,
Of recreations the most innocent,
But now the sport is marde, and wott ye why,
Fishes decrease, and fishers multiply.

Thomas Bastard, English divine, satirist and epigrammatist

THE ADAPTABLE WAGGLER

You might be forgiven for thinking that in coarse fishing, one float is very much like any other. After all it's just that bobbing little rounded stick that anglers pay intense attention to while waiting for a bite. Well no, a float is a bit more than just a sleep-inducing device made to encourage the eyelids to droop. By cunningly adapting the float shape, the angler allows the bait to be presented in many different ways, thereby attracting lots of fish. 'Straight wagglers' (stick-like floats) can in a trice be transformed to make 'body wagglers' called quaintly by such names as 'onions' or 'missiles'. Top match fishermen recommend having separate balsa wood 'bodies' to quickly slip over the straight waggler and transform it into a multitude of luscious shapely forms.

If only we could do the same!

A SMART PARR

If the fry is the baby of the salmon world and the smolt the young immature adult about to migrate to sea to grow, the parr is the pubescent teenager still making his way in river life. Fish breeders will sometimes call them 'precocious parr' meaning they are getting a bit pushy and always trying to carve out their own little niche in the stream. Just like our human teenagers, some fish parr are greedy, inexperienced in life and rather dim in nature. However, others show a remarkably well-developed sense of opportunity. These are indeed the precocious ones, nipping in amongst adult salmon in the act of spawning and shedding their own milt on the female eggs. This is perhaps a way of ensuring that if the old male salmon is not up to the job, the young one is there as a back-up to produce the goods and continue the species. Nature is nothing if not clever.

A KNOTTY PROBLEM

Odd though it may seem, there is almost a cult surrounding fishermen's knots. Here's a list of just some of the most popular:

Blood knot • Needle knot
Loop to loop • Double grinner
Double turle • Blood bight loop
Trilene knot • Blood loop
Tucked half blood • Double blood knot
Figure of eight • Single grinner
Turle knot • Arbor knot
Safe blood knot • Surgeons knot

WALLEYE NEVER

In January 2005, the Rev Mariusz Zajac caught a record walleye (pollack) while ice fishing in his local lake in remote Saskatchewan. At 18.3 pounds this was a new world record for ice-caught walleye and he quickly posted his success on the internet. Unfortunately a prankster, perhaps another angler envious of the catch, then relayed a picture of the Reverend posing with his catch to many different websites, changing the location of the catch each time he sent the picture out. The fish appeared not only to have been caught in Saskatchewan but also Manitoba, Minnesota and then Ontario. Undeterred the good father turned this notoriety on its head by asking anyone who came across his record walleye, genuine or not, to donate a few dollars to the Tsunami Appeal. Most have happily done so and the priest has now become known as the 'fishing father'.

SILLY NONSENSE FISHING

In the best traditions of the late Stanley Unwin these are a few appropriate terms relating to fish and fishing:

Giganterums	Fish that get away
Birdsnesters	Kids who constantly get their line in a tangle
Rumticklers	Fish that nibble but do not swallow the bait
Naglers	Fishermen who are always complaining
Smuttiedutters	Trout which are frustratingly rising to tiny impossible-to-imitate insects
Stickleprats	Very small fish that take your bait when you are after bigger fish
Whizzgons	Bait that falls off the hook immediately you cast it out
Numfiddler	Any piece of equipment that is difficult to operate in cold weather

JUST AN ILLUSION

In the good old days, coarse fishing used to be about catching perhaps a dace or a gudgeon (both not much bigger than a few ounces) on a tiny hook while sitting contemplatively at the side of river or canal. It was a simple, basic skill and you felt mighty proud of what you had achieved. However since the 1980s, coarse fishing has undergone a revolution. The popularity of stocked commercial 'fisheries' – anything from an artificial concrete bowl of a pond to a flooded gravel pit – took off in a big way over 20 years ago and has never looked back. These are now the haunt of the 'nouveau' coarse fisher. Anglers brought up on these fisheries, which are in the main stocked with big carp, largely mock the old ways. Why struggle to get to a quiet spot on the riverbank, search out swims and modify tackle when all you need to do with the new ponds is drive straight to the lakeside, set up shop, switch on your i-Pod and hey presto within five minutes you hook an enormous fish about the size of a small child. Heavy stocking ensures almost without question that you will catch a monster, and quickly too.

Many dedicated fishermen and women are now beginning to think twice about this new fishery ethos. The ability to catch fish, they say, used to require a bit of skill and water craft, but nowadays there doesn't seem to be quite the same challenge involved. They are worried that newcomers to the sport will think that if that's all there is to it, why bother? And they would have a point...

A BIT FISHY

Which is the odd one out?
Ale wife, may fish, chad, houting, King of the Herring.
Answer on page 153.

FOODY FLIES

Crab

Not only do oceanic fish such as bonefish and redfish consume other, smaller fish, but also they like eating crustaceans such as shrimp and small crabs. Designed by American fly fishers who fish predominantly in salt water, these 'flies' – and the term must be used loosely – look remarkably similar to little crawling crustaceans. Patterns known as 'flexo crabs' come complete with beady black eyes, skinny legs and mini pincers, all cleverly fashioned from fur and feather and slipped on to a small hook. Strictly for the specialist, these flies are so cute that they invariably attract plenty of jokes about well-dressed crab.

QUOTE UNQUOTE

Yes, this sport fits me – physically, mentally, psychologically.
Why do I love trout? For the same reasons men do.
Joan Salvato Wulff, widow of Lee Wulff, famous
twentieth-century American angler and fly tyer

THE CORRECTLY DRESSED FLY

In the old days, flies for catching fish were known as 'powerful killers' or 'deadly patterns'; to name a fly with such obvious murderous intent was never considered to be the least bit inappropriate. Nowadays things are different. Here is a fly dressed for our modern, politically correct world:

The politically correct fly

Hook – Biodegradable hand-carved wood not from a rain forest

Tying thread – Cotton from an organically grown crop picked by equal opportunities workers

Body – Unbleached wool from an organically farmed sheep fed on grass grown without pesticides

Wings – Feathers from a corn-fed, free range chicken

Tail – A tuft or two from a bird not on the protected species list

No animals were harmed during the production of this fly

One thing is certain in fishing and that is anglers will never agree. Fishing is steeped with exchanges of view, some gentlemanly but some positively vitriolic. In the nineteenth century, an English angler named Cholmondeley Pennel wrote a book *The Modern Practical Angler*. Pennel was a skilled fisherman, particularly in the art of a wet fly; the black Pennel fly is named after him. However he was none too clever when it came to naming his books. Pennel's tome blatantly copied the title of an already published book *The Practical Angler*, written by that well-respected Scots angler WC Stewart. Not only was the title alike, a good proportion of Pennel's text appeared to be very similar in nature to Stewart's.

Despite protests, the publishers of Pennel's work went ahead and released the book. Immediately they did so, a fierce cross-border war of words erupted. With heated regularity Stewart V Pennel debates followed in that illustrious periodical *The Field* discussing numerous aspects of the two books' similarities. The young Scot flew at Pennel, dander up and hissing that the Englishman's book was: 'A compound of plagiarism, absurdity and self deceit'. Pennel spat back his opinions on Stewart's then modern ideas on fishing a fly upstream: 'In spite of Mr Stewart's able advocacy, most anglers have now arrived at the conclusion that fly fishing up stream always or even generally, is a mistake in practice.'

So intense did their arguing become on the pages of *The Field* that the editor eventually had to call a halt, probably convinced that the protagonists might start another civil war, or at the very least resort to a duel of fly rods at dawn. Many years later, Arthur Ransome, editor of the now defunct *Rod and Line Magazine*, admirably summed up their now faintly ridiculous arguments by stating 'They [Stewart and Pennel] have both been long dead and, I suppose fish the Styx, one fishing up and one fishing down and pass each other without speaking'.

SUPERSTITIONS OF THE SEAFARERS

On the wind

In Caithness in the north of Scotland, sea fishermen of yore had deep superstitions concerning wind or rather that some person wishing them ill could 'whistle up the wind'. The wife of a Caithness fisherman would never blow on any food to cool it down, as it was thought she would cause a storm to rise and endanger her man out at sea. Presumably every time a storm blew up it was immediately the 'her at home's' fault and the seafarers would turn to one another with the desperate cry: 'She's made those cakes again!'.

Cost, in pounds sterling, of an adult season ticket on the Welsh waters of 65 Mawddach and Wnion

STRIPERS FOR EVER

According to the website www.stripersforever.org, the sea-dwelling fish the striped bass is having a bit of a hard time of it. It seems that despite its huge recreational angling popularity, the striper has never been classed as a game fish. This puts it at an immediate disadvantage when it comes to angling availability. The principal reason for this non classification appears to be to safeguard the commercial interests of the trawler fishermen. Each year the trawlermen harvest thousands of these high quality fish, selling them at a high price on the open market. According to www.stripersforever.org, by keeping the sporting anglers interests at bay, the government effectively subsidise the jobs of the commercial fishermen while discouraging recreational angling. Not surprisingly the anglers case is now being more forcibly put to the powers that be with sport fishers claiming that striped bass are the 'peoples fish' and that 'basic freedoms of citizenship' are at stake. Strong stuff – but then anglers do take their sport very seriously...

TERRIBLE FISHING JOKES

A man knocks on the door of a house and says to the woman who opens it: 'Good afternoon, I'm looking for Mr Jones.'

'I'm Mrs Jones,' says the woman. 'Can I help?'

'Oh no,' says the man, 'it's Fishing Club business; can you tell me where I can find him?'

The woman replies: 'Well in that case, take yourself down to the river and look for a stick with a worm at both ends.'

DON'T FORGET YOUR PARACHUTE

According to the *Oxford English Dictionary* a parachute is an apparatus used to check a fall through air and/or descend safely from a great height. When fishing, anglers can use flies made with parachute hackles, which do a similar thing to the descent of a fly as it is cast on to the water. The idea is to tie on feather hackle in such a way that, when finished, the fly looks as if it has its own little personal umbrella attached. The origin of this style of fly tying is obscure, possibly American or Scottish depending on which camp you believe. However English anglers Goddard and Clarke took the design one step further when they made 'upside down' parachute flies. This had the little umbrella parachute on the underside of the hook and, upon landing on the water, the hook point sat up above the water surface. The concept behind this was to fool the trout by keeping the sharp end out of sight. Whether the trout ever noticed this extra subtlety is not known.

Catch of the day.

WHAT ANGLERS SUFFER IN THE NAME OF THEIR SPORT

Limititus

This affliction almost invariably affects reservoir trout fishers. Bag limits are often in force at these fisheries and the angler can become obsessed at making his limit during the allotted time allowed on his day ticket. Quivering wrecks can sometimes be seen towards the day's end thrashing the water to a veritable foam in order to reach the maximum catch limit. Not to do so risks a severely deflated ego and considerable ribbing, if not abject disgrace in the pub afterwards.

The angler rose, he took his rod,
He kneeled and made his prayers to God,
The living God sat overhead:
The angler tripped, the eels were fed.

Robert Louis Stevenson,
The Angler Rose, He Took His Rod

DRESSING A SPIDER

Spiders are not just the dread of the arachnophobe, they are also old traditional types of fly designed to catch trout. In the book *The Practical Angler* written by the famous Scots angler WC Stewart in the 1850s, he describes how to tie a 'spider' 'in hand', a difficult process involving considerable dexterity and patience:

'Dressing a spider is a much simpler operation than dressing a fly, and therefore it is better to begin with it. Having selected a thread of gut and a hook, the next thing is to choose a feather, which to make a neat spider, must be so proportioned to the size of the hook that the legs of the spider, when dressed, will be about the length of the hook. Before commencing, bite the end of the gut between your teeth; this flattens and makes it broader in the point, which prevents it slipping, something very liable to occur with small flies. Next, take the hook firmly between the forefinger and thumb of your left hand, lay the gut along its shank, and with a well-waxed silk thread, commencing about the centre of the hook, whip it and the gut firmly together, till you come to the end of the shank, where form the head by a few turns of the thread. This done, take the feather, and laying it on with the root end towards the bend of the hook, wrap the silk three or four times round it, and then cut off the root end.

'Still holding the hook between the forefinger and thumb of your left hand, take the thread, lay it along the centre of the inside of your feather, and with the forefinger and thumb of your right hand twirl them round together till the feather is rolled round the thread; and in this state wrap it round the hook, taking care that a sufficient number of the fibres stick out to represent the legs; to effect this it will sometimes be necessary to raise the fibres with a needle during the operation. Having carried the feather and thread down to where you commenced, wrap the silk three or four times round the feather, and if there is any left cut it off, and finish with a succession of hitch-knots, or common whip fastening.'

Nowadays, virtually all anglers use a fly tying vice to hold the hook while they add fur and feather, but well might be eternally grateful for a step-by-step picture book.

DIAWL BACH DON'T YOU KNOW

For many years the Welsh fly fishing fraternity rather hid their lights under bushels, and were never as well known in fly tying circles as the English or the Scots. Happily that situation changed for ever in the 1950s when a fly emerged from Wales known as the 'diawl bach'. In Welsh this means 'little devil', an apt name for a pattern that wreaks havoc among trout. This sparse fly, little more than a twist of peacock herl, may have been a long time coming to light, yet the diawl bach is a truly remarkable fly. Not only is it highly successful in Wales, it also catches trout with almost monotonous regularity across the whole of the UK. Few other patterns can claim to be as consistently productive across the country. Anglers from Loch Leven in Scotland to Blagdon Lake in Somerset swear by these flies, which again and again produce the goods in competition fishing. Today, skilled fly fishers will always have a little devil or two in their fly box.

FIRST STEPS IN FISHING

According to the syllabus of the *Scottish Angling Coaching Course (Level 1)* course participants should have knowledge of:

1. Basic health and safety issues
2. Watercraft
3. Overhead casting
4. Roll casting
5. Entomology
6. Fish biology
7. Knot tying
8. The equipment required and where and when it should be used

The course is designed to give training on how to convey the above skills to novice anglers. Sadly, the bit about participants needing a sense of humour is not on the list.

FOODY FLIES

Squid

Forget the chewy calamari so beloved of Spanish restaurants, these flies are made to look like a small but very colourful swimming squid. The flies are used almost exclusively in saltwater fly fishing where 'squids' come in purple, pearl or chartreuse hue. With their impressionistic trailing tentacles made of fine nylon fibres combined with tinsel, beady eyes and longish shiny head, they are said to be very attractive to sea-dwelling fish like barracuda or tarpon, especially if the angler fishes them on a pulsing retrieve, just like the real thing.

Record weight, in pounds, to the nearest pound, of the North American fish, the muskellunge

A Rubby Dubby Cocktail – This is a particularly ghastly bait used in sea fishing. It is not impaled on a hook but is scattered over the side of the boat in order to attract predatory fish into the vicinity. The best Rubby Dubby should be as fresh and as bloody as possible. Use the heads and entrails of newly killed fish like mackerel and mix together in a bucket, then stir well. Though it may attract stubborn resistance, for best results keep the prepared bait cool in the fridge to lessen coagulation. Preparation of Rubby Dubby is not recommended on the morning after a heavy night out.

Extra Warm Extra Wriggly – Freshwater fish can play very hard to get, especially in chilly weather. A maggot or two on the hook of the fly or just on a bare hook can sometimes work wonders. When the conditions are cold, to make the maggots extra-attractive put a few of them in your mouth for a short period to warm them up. This makes them extra-wriggly, which fish find exciting. Avoiding swallowing may be sensible.

Bed inspections – Oceanic fish love rag worm particularly king rag, but the bait needs lots of TLC to stay in good condition. Pick out any damaged bodies from your freshly dug-up rags, wrap them in newspaper and inspect frequently for signs of a squidgy damp mess. Change the bed daily until all excess moisture is absorbed. This keeps your king rags happy for weeks, lucky them.

QUOTE UNQUOTE

Angling may be said to be so like the mathematics,
that it can never be fully learnt.
Izaak Walton, author of *The Compleat Angler*

DUBLIN'S NOT SO FAIR

Late in 2004 the Irish Central Fisheries Board had to carry out an emergency rescue of more than 10,000 distressed fish from the Grand Canal Basin in Dublin. An accidental sewage discharge into a section of the waterway caused thousands of fish to go belly up. The Fisheries Board rescuers worked frantically to shift eels, perch, pike and roach to a non-polluted part of the upper canal. In a scene reminiscent of a fishy *ER*, rescue efforts involved giving the gasping fish oxygen via an aerated tank, before transferring them to safer waters. Although many fish did die, the dramatic salvage eventually proved worthwhile, as over 10,000 fish lived to enjoy their new and less polluted home.

A BIT FISHY

Name six species of fish ending in '-ing'.
Answer on page 153.

ENTER THE ROBOTIC FISH

Professor Jens Blachen of the Norwegian University of Science and Technology at Trondheim has come up with a novel remote controlled 'cyberfish' which is going to give us an inside view of the problems fish are facing in the world's oceans. The device literally swims with the fish in their unique shoals and relays its data electronically. Apparently Professor Balchens team have so far learned that regarding navigation and avoiding predators, salmon are distinctly dim, cod are stubborn and difficult to steer but the humble coley (saithe) is by far the smartest of the subjects tested so far.

A LITERARY CATCH

Ursula: The pleasant'st angling is to see the fish
      Cut with her golden oars the silver stream
      And greedily devour the treacherous bait.
      So angle we for Beatrice, who even now
      Is couch'd in the woodbine coverture.

                      Much Ado About Nothing,
                      William Shakespeare

SPEAR IT IN

A peculiar form of big game fishing has grown up in antipodean waters. Instead of anglers sitting with a cold beer sunny Caribbean style on plush yachts, anglers have taken to getting in the water with their prospective catch. Their intentions are not benign, however, for they take with them a powerful spear gun. Apparently there are now hotly contested Spearfishing Championships held in Australian and NZ waters. Anglers – or should they be called divers – are allowed only a wet suit, snorkel, mask and a gun equipped with float and line. They must spear the fish and then land it by bringing it to the surface and boating it without the aid of scuba-diving equipment. Target fish species are normally local fish like porae or kahawhai but occasionally bigger fish like marlin are landed. In 1997 a marlin of nearly 300 pounds was speared and after an epic tussle was eventually landed. Larger marlin have been taken since. What Hemingway would have thought of this is anyone's guess.

FISHERS' COMPLAINTS

Anglers are notorious for complaining about the weather; no matter what the weather, there's always something wrong with it, such as:

It's too bright
It's too cold
It's too hot
It's too wet
It's too dry
It's too windy
It's too still
The water's too high
The water's too low
The water's too clear
The water's too coloured

ANGLING PLOYS THAT DIDN'T CATCH ON

Needle-eyed hooks

In the late nineteenth century, the making of fishhooks reached new heights of design with 'up eyes' and 'down eyes' being crafted on to the (blunt) end of the hook to enable anglers to tie hook to line securely. Needle-eyed hooks with an eye cut through the end of the hook shank like a needle were made for a time, but anglers quickly gave up on them due to their excessive awkwardness.

VIRTUALLY CAUGHT

The 2005 Miami Boat Show featured a fishing competition sponsored by such diverse organisations as the International Bill Fish Network, Scopinich Fighting Chairs and the American Fisheries Society. Nothing unusual in that you might think; except that the competition took place indoors, there was no sea spray, no fish were really caught and no blood was shed. Despite this odd setting, competitors still won angling accolades, for what they were participating in is a novel sport known as virtual big game fishing. Anglers have just less than two and a half minutes to try and land a monster cyber sailfish. The competitors are strapped into a fighting chair, given a digitally controlled fishing rod and reel and watch a film on a monitor in front of them. The clever part is the weight on the line they have to wind in, which acts in time with the leaping sailfish on the screen. Apparently the participant gets a great workout without ever coming into contact with the real thing. And it's good for fish conservation, too.

MOST IRRITATING EVENTS DURING FISHING EXPEDITIONS

1. You lose the fish of a lifetime, in front of an audience comprising of town drunks and small boys.

2. You try to reach a little further and snag your cast in a tree either in front or behind; both have equal annoyance ratings.

3. You walk for miles to reach the remotest water of your dreams only to open the tackle bag and find you have forgotten the reel.

4. You shut the rod in the car door before or after going fishing (before is worse).

5. You jump in the car and drive off, straight over the reel or the rod or both.

6. You drive home with the rod sticking out of the window, the line catches in a tree and whizzes out behind you leaving a lengthy and expensive trail of knitting.

QUOTE UNQUOTE

Dr Johnson and Lord Byron, these famed fondlings of their age, have said some smart things to render angling ridiculous as a pastime.
John Younger, nineteenth-century angler

WHAT'S WILD?

Anglers speak about wild trout in tones of deep reverence. Normally they are referring to trout that have procreated naturally in a wild setting. These trout must be distinguished, however, from 'native' fish, which are the original colonisers from the last Ice Age. Because of the amount of stocking of trout (grown in hatchery tanks) into waters containing native fish, a practice begun in Victorian times and still going on today, many ancient gene lines have been corrupted. Thus many rivers and lakes that are described as containing wild trout actually contain fish of extremely mixed bloodlines, while native trout waters contain the pure non-genetically modified versions. These fragile fish populations (mainly occurring in Scotland) are the ones that need to be carefully conserved, for they are at the centre of our angling heritage.

Gravel-voiced George Melly freely admits to having been so excited about catching a wild trout he had to dash into the bushes and masturbate with a dock leaf. Who knows what he would have done if he'd hooked a native...

Cleopatra: Give me mine angle. Well to th'river. There,
My music playing far off, I will betray
Tawny – skinned fishes. My bending hook shall pierce
Their slimy jaws, and as I draw them up
I'll think every one of them an Antony,
And say, Ah ha, you're caught!

William Shakespeare, *Antony and Cleopatra*

OTHER NAMES FOR WRIGGLY THINGS USED AS BAIT

1. Gozzers
2. Pinkies
3. Casters
4. Squatts
5. Rags
6. King rags
7. Black lugs
8. Yellow tail lugs
9. Sewie
10. Well worms
11. Blow lugs
12. Red lugs
13. Soft lugs
14. Harbour rags

ALL THE BETTER TO SEE YOU WITH

Swordfish, tuna and marlin native to the Pacific Ocean have been found to have the capacity to improve their vision by using what could only be described as centrally-heated eyeballs. Apparently they have a specially adapted heating organ in the muscle adjacent to their large tennis ball shaped eyes. This has the effect of warming their eyes, which in turn greatly enhances their ability to spot their prey at greater distances. It would seem evolution of the species has produced specially tailored retinas, which when heated allow the swordfish to capture the available light more quickly and see better what might be trying to escape its jaws. This phenomenon is even odder when you consider the rest of the fish's body remains cold-blooded. Big game fishermen can take heart that although the fish see their prey better, heated eyeballs do not help them to distinguish between real food and the anglers' artificial lures.

74 *Cost in pounds sterling, times a million, of salmon and sea trout fishing to the Scottish economy in 2003*

SCOTLAND'S ALL-BUT-FORGOTTEN TWENTIETH-CENTURY FISHING HEROES

RC Bridgett

During the latter half of the nineteenth century it became fashionable among the angling intelligentsia to deride the sport of trout loch fishing as greatly inferior when compared to the same sport done on a river. Basically, their reasoning boiled down to some ill-informed thinking mixed with a fair bit of 'lowland' versus 'highland' snobbery. Bridgett saw this with astute clarity and did much to reverse the trend. He wrote most of his books in the 1920s, of which *Loch Fishing in Theory and Practice* was the most erudite and the most successful. Bridgett is most famous for dispelling what he called 'a charge against the loch'. Though few modern anglers remember him now, Bridgett's lucid writings have gone a long way towards helping loch anglers to go about their business without feeling little better than lepers.

DEATH BY FISHING

Warning: do NOT try this to see if it works – it does!

1. Find the nearest electricity pylon and/or power line to the river or lake
2. Stand under it, preferably in the water with metal-studded boots
3. Select a lead core line
4. Use a long carbon fibre rod – at least 15 foot is recommended
5. Cast vigorously with a high arm action

SYMBOLIC FISH

Fish drawings, motifs or symbols crop up again and again throughout history, sometimes as mere decoration, and also sometimes as meaningful symbols. The Romans adorned their villa walls with ornate drawings of decorative fish while the early Christians adopted the fish more as a religious symbol, which has endured until the present day. The Normans featured fish in their architecture and monuments, while the Anglo Saxons had fish emblazoned on anything from swords to drinking vessels. At this time the fish seem to be there more as something nice to look at rather than a definite symbol. In contrast during the eighth century AD the untameable Picts of northern Scotland erected their Pictish stones and these feature fish symbols the meaning of which is lost in antiquity.

It was not until Dame Juliana Berners's *The Treatise of Fishing with an Angle* was published in 1496, that we see fish and angling connected in an arty drawing on the frontispiece of this book. And the rest as they say is history...

COMPLETELY BIASED LIST OF
WONDERFUL FISHING WRITERS

Harry Plunket Greene – Plunket did most of his fishing on the Hampshire chalkstreams, notably the River Bourne during the 1920s. He was an accomplished professional singer as well as a master of the printed word, capable of making fishing seem witty, beautiful and intriguing all at the same time. His seminal book *Where Bright Waters Meet* was written in between his operatic recitals and can be read again and again without boredom.

Hugh Falkus – Falkus was a forthright character well known in twentieth century angling circles for suffering few fools gladly, yet his angling writing manages to combine boundless practical insight with grace and wit. His heyday of fishing was in the 1970s when he made the English border Esk River his own. When not fishing, Falkus made TV documentaries principally on animal behaviour and natural history and it is his voice you hear narrating classic wildlife programmes such as *The World About Us* and *The Undersea World of Jacques Cousteau*.

TC Kingsmill Moore – the late KM was an esteemed judge in the Irish High Court and this is only too apparent in his writing, which was sharply observant and astute yet completely without verbosity. His fishing career spanned more than 50 years from the 1920s to the 1970s and his book *A Man May Fish* is probably the best on Irish sea trout fishing ever written.

GM Skues – Skues was a successful barrister of the late nineteenth century who eagerly applied his shrewd analysing skills to trout angling. His far thinking 'nymph' fishing theories were mainly conducted on the chalkstreams of Hampshire and these formed a backdrop to his taking on the might of Halford's dry fly establishment. This was a prolonged and at times quite vicious 'wet versus dry fly' argument, spanning 20 years or more. Skues eventually won the day while still managing to write lyrically and without bitterness on the sport he loved so much.

John Inglis Hall – Inglis Hall is a writer in the Plunket Greene mode, gently funny yet involving and inspiring. This was an Englishman who became passionate about the remote little River Truim in the wild highlands of Scotland fishing it ardently from the early 1950s. The result of this loving research was the little book *Fishing a Highland Stream – A Love Affair with a River*, a timeless work and a sheer joy to read.

'Scuse me Sir but can I have a bigger rod?

BRITAIN'S FISHING FASHIONS

Scottish wets

Scotland may often be wet and windy but it's also the traditional home of what is known as wet fly fishing. Wet flies are the ones that sink below the water surface and Scots have fished with these patterns since the nation first embraced the art of fly fishing in the nineteenth century, if not earlier. This method of fishing suits the Scottish temperament to a tee; canny, searching and methodical. When executed skillfully, wet fly fishing on river and loch thoroughly covers all angles and depths. Few trout can resist the lure of a well-presented wet Dunkeld, Clan Chief or Loch Ordie, flies not quite with kilts on but close enough.

MEANEST FISH PREDATORS

Both freshwater and oceanic fish suffer from predation. For example the cormorant eats 25% of its own body weight in fish every day while seals consume anything from 10% to 20% of their body weight in fish per day. Predators like the non-native mink or signal crayfish, having been brought to the UK for sources of fur and food respectively, escape or are deliberately released from captivity. Once in the wild they breed quickly and consume huge amounts of small fish fry and fish eggs, which is bad news for fish stocks. Here are 10 of the worst fish-eating culprits:

1. Cormorants
2. Seals
3. Pike
4. American Signal Crayfish
5. Mink
6. Otters (but we forgive them)
7. Zander
8. Mergansers
9. Grass snakes
10. Ospreys (we let them off too)

QUOTE UNQUOTE

The employment of fishing seems to be a great bar to industry in other branches, as it partakes too much of the nature of sport, as well as of labour.
The *First Statistical Account of Scotland* of 1973

REEL IT IN

The earliest reports of using a reel when out fishing, something all anglers now take for granted, come from the early seventeenth century. Prior to that time the fishing line (usually made of horsehair) was simply tied on to the end of the rod. The first reels were terribly basic affairs also known as winders and winches. In Scotland a reel was known as a 'pirn'. In game fishing, reels were first introduced to assist the catching of salmon. Some method of storing and controlling the running line during the playing of a large thrashing fish was deemed essential and the reel was born. Trout fishers cottoned on to the device a little later but by the end of the nineteenth century most freshwater anglers were using reels made of brass or wood. From then until now the phrases 'reel it in' or 'wind it in' took over from 'haul it in' which referred more to pulling up a net than applying the rod.

STICK AN OAR IN

In 2004 a woman angler busy fishing for cod with squid bait off the Cleveland coast of north east England caught and landed a scarce monster of the deep; an oarfish weighing 63.5 kilogrammes and measuring 3.5 metres long. The fish weighed 13 kilogrammes more than the angler did. Unfortunately scientists were left bitterly disappointed as, before they could get there and, perhaps not realising the rarity of the catch, the woman sliced it up and put it in her freezer. Sadly, oarfish are plankton feeders and are flavourless fish. They do not make good eating. It is not known if the household are still munching their way through the oarfish – grilled, boiled, barbecued, fried, baked...

WHAT THE FLOAT DOES

- Shows you when a fish bites
- Helps you cast further
- Holds the bait in the swim
- Helps control of the line
- Sometimes attracts fish to the bait
- Helps you land a fish by guiding it away from weed
- Helps you fish in the dark when it has a lighted top

A LITERARY CATCH

Thus as the angler looks back he thinks less of individual captures and days than of the scenes in which he fished. The luxuriance of water meadows animated by insect and bird and trout life, tender with the green and gay blossoms of early spring: the nobleness and volume of great salmon rivers: the exhilaration of looking at any salmon pool, great or small; the rich brownness of highland water: the wild openness of treeless, trackless spaces which he has traversed in an explorer's spirit of adventure to search likely water for sea trout: now on one, now on another of these scenes the angler's mind will dwell, as he thinks of fishing. Special days and successes he will no doubt recall, but always with the remembrance and the mind's vision of the scenes and the world in which he fished. For, indeed, this does seem a separate world, a world of beauty and enjoyment. This time must come to all of us, who live long, when memory is more than prospect. An angler who has reached this stage and reviews the pleasure of life will be grateful and glad he has been an angler, for he will look back upon days radiant with happiness, peaks and peaks of enjoyment that are not less bright because they are lit in memory by the light of a setting sun.

Sir Edward Grey, *Fly Fishing*

A BIT FISHY

What are 'agile darters' and 'laboured swimmers'?
Answer on page 153.

CORACLES

The coracle is one devilish form of water transportation. One false move and it tips you in the drink. Nevertheless the Welsh have persevered with this small personal boat for many centuries. The coracle has a rounded wooden frame covered with an animal skin and looks rather like an upturned turtle shell. The fisherman sits on one single seat in the interior and propels himself along with a very basic oar, little more than a plank of wood. Rod fishing is not much done from the coracle as they are extremely light and unstable craft and any enthusiastic casting is more likely to see you swimming; instead, fishermen have traditionally strung a net between two coracles and hauled in the fish in this way. Fishers take their coracle to the river by carrying it on their back. They are easily recognised as they look like a very large beetle walking on two legs.

TERRIBLE FISHING JOKES

Two anglers were chatting away as they made their way to the riverbank. 'Oh I love fishing,' said one. 'The fresh air. The solitude. The birds singing, the sunsets. It's man against nature, pitting your wits with denizens of the deep. The thrill of catching a fish and the battle to land a crafty adversary. Tell me. Why do you go fishing?'

'My daughter's learning to play the violin.'

CORK BUTTS

The butt of a rod, the section an angler holds in order to cast the line was, prior to the 1880s, integral to the rod, with the wood hewn into a cigar shape for the angler to hold. The wealthier angler might have this covered with pigskin for added comfort. After 1900 the rod makers imported cork from Portugal, usually in a wrap-around strip form. This had the advantage of making the rod considerably lighter and was softer to the touch. Ground cork of poorer quality was used to make the butt on less expensive rods. The phrase 'give it some butt' sounds like encouraging an aggressive playing of the fish; however, it actually means arching the rod back over the shoulder and showing the butt end of the rod to the fish. This affords the angler better control of the struggle ensuing at the end of the line.

FISHING ON THE TELLY

Despite the huge popularity of fishing as a sport (there are at least three million anglers in the UK who fish regularly), dedicated fishing programmes are mainly confined to satellite TV. This list features some of the current and some of the oft repeated:

Angling Times TV
Bueno Vista
Day Ticket
Fishing on the Edge
Go Fishing
Great Rod Race
Hooked on Fishing
Irish Pike on the Fly
Jungle Hooks
Main Stream
A Passion for Angling
Predators
Rex Hunt's Fishing Adventures
Screaming Reels
Total Fishing

QUOTE UNQUOTE

A sly old fish, too cunning for the hook.
George Crabbe, writer of *The Parish Register*.

SPINNING AROUND

When anglers talk about spinning or spinners, they could be talking about either of two things. On the one hand spinners can be those fishy shapes made of shiny metal with a mean looking treble hook on the end. You will see anglers using short rods to whiz their spinner out attached to clear monofilament line. Having cast out, it's just a question of reeling it back in furiously while hoping an unsuspecting fish will snap up the spinner either in a fit of pique or because they think it's a rapidly escaping prey. This simple fishing ploy is known as spinning. But the other kind of spinner is of a much more delicate nature. Spinners in fly fishing are the filmy adult version of an up-winged fly like a Blue Winged or Large Dark Olive. Fly fishers revere these flies and make elegant imitations of spinners as trout love them. Quite how the insect got its name is a little unclear but it would seem to be something to do with the behaviour of the fluttery dancing clouds of these insects, often seen busily 'spinning' above river pools on warm evenings.

FISHES YOU MAY NOT HAVE HEARD OF

1. Bitterling – This is a small pretty-coloured fish with a deep blue-green sheen running along a flank of pink to light purple hue. It was first introduced to Britain in the 1920s, probably from eastern Asia to stock ornamental fish ponds. Bitterling are found in only a few select waters in Britain, mainly in the Midlands. Despite their scarcity they have a hardy constitution and are able to survive in murky waters, where most other species would go belly up.

2. Sunbleak – Another small rather cute looking fish with silvery flanks, green back and a blue sheen along its sides, the sunbleak is found at only a few sites in south west England. Sunbleak are not native to Britain and were first introduced in 1986 in the Hampshire area as ornamental fish. Because they are bossy little creatures which breed abundantly they are not welcome in UK waters where native fish populations exist.

3. Pumkinseed – A peculiar looking small fish rather like a mean looking goldfish with spiky fins and dusky bars along a deep flank of bronze laced with irregular blue green lines. The pumkinseed is an alien species introduced from America in the early 1900s. The fish prefer still waters and their presence is said to be spreading in waters in southern England where they are now considered a pest.

FAMOUS LADIES IN FISHING

Dame Diana Rigg

Esteemed British actress who, when not treading the boards, spends as much time as possible wafting a fly rod. Having begun her fishing career literally learning her (fishing) lines on the River Teith in Stirlingshire, she quickly took to engaging in the theatre of streams and remains a staunch fan of British game fishing.

PURE PISCES

According to the website www.astroagency.com a person born under the star sign Pisces likes the element of water, exhibits changeable qualities, has negative polarity, is careless and secretive but can be friendly and receptive at the same time. Pisceans generally show a bit of a split personality, sometimes outgoing to the point of recklessness yet on other occasions they remain quietly introverted. Their 'keywords' are sensitivity, sympathy, inspiration and flight. Apparently there is a deep-rooted nature in Pisceans to flee any scene they find a bit uncomfortable – in other words they appear easily spooked. A bit like fish then...

Estimated cost, in millions of pounds sterling, of carp-lover Freddie Mercury's estate in 2005

A LITERARY CATCH

You strange, astonished-looking, angel-faced,
Dreary-mouthed, gaping wretches of the sea,
Gulping salt-water everlastingly,
Cold-blooded, though with red your blood be graced,
And mute, though dwellers in the roaring waste;
And you, all shapes beside, that fishy be,
Some round, some flat, some long, all devilry,
Legless, unloving, infamously chaste:

O scaly, slippery, wet, swift, staring wights,
What is't ye do? What life lead? eh, dull goggles?
How do ye vary your vile days and nights?
How pass your Sundays? Are ye still but joggles
In ceaseless wash? Still nought but gapes, and bites,
And drinks, and stares, diversified with boggles?

James Henry Leigh Hunt,
To a Fish

MATERIALS THAT HAVE BEEN
USED TO MAKE FISHING RODS

Ash • Bamboo cane • Blackthorn
Carbon Fibre • Crab tree
Fibre Glass • Greenheart
Hazel • Hickory • Lancewood
Whalebone • Willow • Yew

PHISHING PIRANHAS

In the twenty-first century a new and distinctly nasty form of fishing has appeared, which bears no relation to Walton's gentle art. The intention of phishing (the deliberately misspelled name was coined by a computer hacker in the 1990s) is to strip bank accounts clean by using various forms of internet scams. The phisher sends out falsified email requests by banks and other institutions to any computer owner, telling them they must update their customer details. If the unsuspecting prey is caught out by these requests and enters his or her credit card or bank account details, the phisher moves in like the piranha and strips their bank account down to its bare bones in seconds. If you get a similar request from a phishing piranha, like all good anglers you should throw it back into the cybersea by pressing the delete button.

TERRIBLE FISHING JOKES

It was a boiling hot day on the local river. An old man stood fishing from the bank looking weary and disconsolate. A young fellow angler passing stopped and asked: 'Any luck?' The old man just heaved a heavy sigh. 'Why don't you take a break and come to the pub with me and we'll have a beer,' the young man offered. They made their way to the nearby hostelry and the younger angler bought the old man a foaming pint of ice cold ale.

'Tell me,' he said, 'have you caught anything today at all?'

The old man turned to him and gave a wry grin. 'You're the fourth,' he said.

LIES, DAMNED LIES AND STATISTICS

1 In Britain in 2003 over 4.2 million people had been fishing within the two previous years, according to the UK Environment Agency. That's 7% of the population with an angling interest.

2 In the USA, 16% or 34 million American anglers over the age of 15 went fishing in 2001 and spent over 36 billion dollars on the sport, according to a US National Survey.

3 In Europe, 5% of the total population of 20 countries in Europe went angling at least once in 2003, according to the European Anglers Alliance.

QUOTE UNQUOTE

It was this big.
Nick Fisher's favourite phrase in TV series *Screaming Reels*

TO SKIN A FISH

Recent developments in tanning procedures have meant that normally discarded fish skins from species like salmon, stingray, shark or cod are being recycled and made into fish leather products. Manufacturers are now able to produce a range of fish skin apparel and accessories which are said to match the durable qualities of crocodile leather, while having a similar softness and texture to manmade fibres. Famous fashion houses like Dior have experimented with pink salmon shoes, Bottega Veneta retailed stingray clutch bags for over a thousand dollars and salmon bikinis have been marketed by Skini, the Scottish fashion house. Ireland, France, Canada, USA and New Zealand have already got in on the recycling act and manufacturers are hoping to hook up with plenty of new customers and land some lucrative sales orders.

A BIT FISHY

What was the 'carshalton dodge'?
Answer on page 153.

SALMON IN A BASKET

One of the first methods used to catch a salmon was not by rod and line but by using a wicker basket. This would be placed in the river below a waterfall. Salmon running up the river would try and leap the falls and those that were not successful fell back into the waiting basket below. At one time at the falls of Arkaig, near the country estate house of Achnacarry, the resident cook had an ingenious early warning rope system installed. If a salmon landed in the basket, the weight of the fish pulled on the rope, which activated a bell in the kitchen. Cook would then know that salmon was going to be the main dish on the menu that evening.

FILMS WITH SOMETHING FISHY IN THEM

A Fish called Wanda
A River Runs Through It
Free Willy
Jaws
Little Mermaid
Piranha
Shark Tale
20,000 Leagues Under the Sea

LONG ISLAND ON THE LINE

Anglers and commercial fishermen of Long Island Sound, off the eastern seaboard of America are up in arms at the prospect of a huge floating liquid gas terminal being set in the midst of their fish-rich waters. According to the website www.savethesound.org, the area is one of the most important bodies of water in the USA. It is home to thousands of species of wildlife and fish and provides employment and recreational opportunities for millions of people in the region. Should the development get the go-ahead the area will be transformed with a 10 storey terminal the length of four football pitches that will dominate the skyline. Fishermen will also have their access cut dramatically in the area not to mention the potential for pollution from the plant. On the one hand environmentalists claim the facility will threaten human and ecological safety; on the other developers say it will do no such thing. With no common ground anywhere it looks as if this argument will run and run.

Since the 1960s, when stocks of game fish such as wild salmon began to seriously diminish, there has been an ongoing dilemma in the sport of game fishing. It involves killing (or not, as the case may be). On the one hand anglers like to see themselves as skilled hunters stalking their prey as our ancestors did. We learn skills that allow us to land the fly inches from the salmon's nose, we spend long hours studying watercraft and getting to know about the habits of fish. We make shedloads of mistakes but eventually we learn enough from our experiences to be able to really know what we are doing. Then we creep up along the river, select a likely spot, launch a handmade fly so convincing that a salmon takes a pop at it and, bingo, we have the catch. All our inherited genes tell us we should bear the prize home for our family to admire and more importantly to eat. We are proud of our achievements in providing food for the home, and rightly so.

The antithesis of this behaviour is the modern ethos that, having struggled sometimes for years to catch your prized wild salmon, you should then put it back.

Anglers call this 'Catch and Release', and of all the fishing methods this is presently one of the most controversial. The aim is undoubtedly laudable – having caught the salmon, you return it to the wild to go on and continue the species. But many anglers think this a weak conservation measure, put in place only after centuries of over-fishing by other people. The trouble is that salmon fishing was and still is big business. Many anglers feel that if river fishery owners had not allowed so much over-exploitation in the past of salmon at sea and in the river, then today's angler probably wouldn't have to throw back his catch of a lifetime. The other argument is that you can buy farmed salmon over the counter so cheaply that you don't need to take a fresh wild salmon home as food. Which is fine if you don't mind eating fish that often has all the excitement of a flaccid and greasy piece of rubber.

So it seems that modern game anglers are now paying the price for others' past greed, and while the proud hunter has not quite disappeared, he is now confined to the fishing minority.

A LITERARY CATCH

P.S. Can you tell me, you who have so watched all sea creatures, whether male Crustaceans ever fight for the females: is the female sex in the sea, like on the land, 'teterrima belli causa'? I beg you not to answer this letter, without you can & will be so kind as to tell about Crustacean Battles, if such there be.

From a letter written by Charles Darwin
to Philip Henry Gosse, 27 April 1857

I knew I shouldn't have asked him to pass the salt.

QUOTE UNQUOTE

Sometimes, in spite of all odds, the bungler gains the day.
Sir John Colquhoun, nineteenth-century sportsman and angler

THE END OF THE KING

The kelt is the end of the line for a male Atlantic salmon. Having survived the rigours of growing up in a British river, migrated to sea, travelled thousands of miles to deep water feeding grounds off Greenland, fed and grown there, returned to its natal river and outlasted all the mean predators along the way, the kelt has spawned with a female salmon and is pretty much on its last legs as it slowly drops back to sea. During this time his condition has been transformed from a spanking athletic bright silver bar to a pathetic-looking creature with flaccid flesh, dull colour and a sad, gaunt scraggy appearance. Many, if not most of these male fish do not make it back to the sea and collapse and die in the river, a sad end to a proud magnificent fish. The remainder that begin to recover in freshwater take on a silvery appearance and from a distance look like fresh-run fish. Anglers catching these fish should by law gently return them with the respect such an extraordinary fish deserves.

Bright eggs

In the 1990s the idea emerged in America that it might be good to dress up a fly to look like an egg, and, more particularly, a salmon egg. Trout and sea trout are very partial to snaffling up these brightly coloured eggs after the salmon have gone about their spawning business; the trout find that they add a tasty dose of protein and fat to their normal insect diet. Cunning anglers worked out that if they could fashion an orange or yellow ball of fluff on a hook they might have a good chance of catching a greedy trout. While that might sound simple, the first 'eggs' tied were poor efforts which slid off the hook (you try tying a ball of fur on a skinny shank, it's just not that easy). Nevertheless, the American fly tyers persevered and anglers in the UK now use 'eggs' of all colour and hue, including sparkly hot pink and crystal chartreuse.

MAIN CAUSES OF DEGRADATION OF FRESHWATER FISH HABITAT

1. Abstraction of water for human consumption
2. Livestock grazing and incursion into water courses
3. Afforestation in areas where fish would normally spawn
4. Agricultural practices particularly drainage ditching
5. Industrial effluent discharges
6. Road workings adjacent to the watercourse
7. Sewage discharge near estuarine habitats

SALMON AND SASSENACHS – SHOW US YOUR GOLD

In 1429 the ninth parliament of James I passed an Act which detailed various measures on salmon preservation. However, written into its midst was a distinct bias towards the Scottish fish merchants of this era. The Act stated 'It is ordained that no Scottish man sell to Englishmen, or in England beforehand or otherwaies, ony salmonde, bot that Englishmen bye them in Scotland for English gold, and none other contentation.' It then went on to advocate that if the English would not buy Scottish salmon in Scotland that 'the Scottish merchandes may sell them in Flanders or other places, quhair them thinkis; swa that of wise they nouther send them nor sell them in England.' Thus James I ensured that the English would always have to travel to Scotland to buy their salmon and thereby probably created one of the first monopoly fish markets in Britain.

88 *Cost, to the nearest pound sterling, of a 32-compartment Wheatley fly box in 2005*

Various tongue-twisting Gaelic names for lochs occur across the length and breadth of Scotland, the waters are usually so named because of their distinguishing features. Interpreting a name will sometimes aid your final decision on whether the loch is going to be worth the long tramp out to fish it, or not.

Here are a few examples of common loch names:

Loch Clach or **Nan Clach** – A stony loch. Often refers to a boulder-strewn shoreline and might mean difficult wading. Check for other clues as to the nature of the environment, however, as sometimes infertile stony-looking waters hold big fish, especially if they are spring-fed.

Loch Beg – A little loch. A very common loch name in Scotland and only gives an indication of water size rather than fishing quality.

Loch Fada – Means a long loch and it's going to be a long stretch of water to cover.

Loch Mhor or **Lloch More** – A big loch.

Loch na Moine – Loch of the bog, probably with a distinctly difficult squidgy shoreline and dark peaty water. Quality rating doubtful and trout in acidic water tend to remain small throughout their adult lives.

Loch Nam Breac – Breac is the Gaelic word for trout and therefore this loch is likely to hold a reasonable supply of them. Always worth a cast.

Loch Meadie or **Loch Caol** – both these names mean a narrow loch where your neighbour on the far shore is always in view.

HERON THE HUNTER

The traditional method by which a heron catches its prey is by standing rock-still on one leg, head on one side, stealthily stalking the unsuspecting fish that is quietly minding its own business in the pool below. In a blink of that wickedly beady black eye, the heron shoots its long neck out, seizes the fish in its beak and with a quick toss of the head, the poor fish is dispatched straight down the bird's gullet. Now according to a recently published survey led by the McGill University in Montreal, Canada, researchers have found herons have 'learned' fly fishing techniques. Birds have apparently been sighted catching flies in their beaks, dropping them like an artificial fly upon the surface of the water and then waiting for a fish to rise to the bait, whereupon the smart heron swallows it whole.

Prior to the days of the internet, fishing magazines thrived. Some still do but a good many have sunk without trace.

First a few of the live ones:

American Angler
American Fly Fisher
Anglers Mail
Angling Times
Coarse Fisherman
Field & Stream
Fly Fishing & Fly Tying
Improve your Coarse Fishing
Sea Angler
Trout Fisherman
Trout & Salmon

And a few of the casualties:

Countrysport
Fishing Gazette
Game Gazette
Rod and Line
Salmon Trout & Sea Trout
Scottish Angler
Strike!
Total Fly Fisher
Waterlog

JOHN GIERACH, ALL AMERICAN ANGLER

Thirty years ago, no angler had ever heard of John Gierach. Nowadays his 14 or so books have achieved worldwide recognition, and sit somewhere between the off beat and the instructional with more than a hint of cult status about them. With appealingly quirky titles like *Sex, Death and Flyfishing*, *Trout Bum* and *Standing in a River Waving a Stick* already under his belt, it's perhaps not surprising that Gierach is a bestseller. As well as books he also writes regular columns for the illustrious magazine *Fly Rod and Reel (FFR)*. In an interview with the e-zine www.midcurrent.com the editor of *FFR*, Paul Guernsey, said of Gierach: 'John is the angling voice of his generation, he is probably the best known fly fisherman in the country next to Lefty Kreh. His sense of irony and introspection is outstanding and he is a very authentic, very American writer'.

And who are we to argue...

QUOTE UNQUOTE

Fhuair e air falbh.
'It got away', in Gaelic

FLIES WITH INNUENDO

Boobies

Rainbow trout are particularly partial to 'boobies', but then they are not known to have graduated much past a 'page three' brain anyway. Boobies are best described as corruptions of already existing artificial fly patterns. You can make just about any large fly or lure into a booby by dressing it up with two balls of ethafoam. For maximum effect (and I kid you not) the little balls have to be encased in ladies' stockings. You then place the snug packages at either side of the head of the fly. The protuberances make the fly extra buoyant and it jiggles and bounces around on the top of the waves, literally taking on the appearance of the 'Fallen Madonna with the big ones'. It is so successful that sometimes the trout seem to be squabbling as they try to get at the buxom fly, and appear to push each other out of the way.

A LITERARY CATCH

For angling-rod he took sturdy oak;
For line, a cable that in storm ne'er broke;
His hook was such as heads the end of pole,
To pluck down house ere fire consumes it whole;
This hook was bated with a dragon's tail,
And then on rock he stood to bob for whale.

Sir William Davenant, *Brittania Triumphans*

HORSES FOR COURSES

The delicate seahorse is one heck of a strange fish. If you look at one closely, you'll see that its strange shape is actually that of a deformed fish, made that way by thousands of years of evolution. Its tail alone is a clever piece of work. No other fish in the ocean has a prehensile tail, which acts as an arm to hold them steady in the current; squid and cuttlefish have tentacles, but these are not the same. But the really special thing about the seahorse is the fact that the males give birth and not the females. The male carries and incubates the eggs, which the female deposits in his abdominal pouch, for about six weeks and then goes into labour. Two hundred baby sea horses later he's finished, while the female is nowhere to be seen. How smart is that...

Most anglers know of the Environment Agency (EA) because in England and Wales, they must pay their rod licence fees direct to this government-led organisation. However the EA is not just a licence fee collector, but the principal body for the protection and enhancement of the environment. It has no jurisdiction in Scotland where a number of bodies exist to oversee different aspects of the environment including, amongst others, the Scottish Environmental Protection Agency (SEPA) and Scottish National Heritage (SNH).

According to their website *www.environment-agency.gov.uk*, the EA has the laudable aim of 'contributing to the sustainable development and integrated management of air, land and water thus ensuring a better quality of life for everyone, now and for generations to come'. The Agency has specific responsibilities regarding the management of fisheries in terms of conservation, recreation, pollution prevention and control, waste management, flood defence and navigation of waterways. A wide-ranging not to say challenging remit perhaps, but at least fish are rightfully acknowledged as key indicators of the state of rivers and lakes. After all, it is fish who are the first to go belly up should a body of water become polluted in some way. With this in mind one of the principal aims of the EA is to help ensure healthy and abundant freshwater fish stocks and populations. They do this by:

- Controlling the fishing pressure on waters through the issuing of the national rod licence and making relevant bylaws. These local fishery laws can cover anything from times of fishing to methods of angling. For example, fly fishing might be allowed but bait angling not.

- Ensuring the health and abundance of fish stocks by the regular surveying of fisheries.

- Preventing damage to fish and fish stocks by effective legal enforcement of fishery laws.

- Rescuing fish when pollution incidents occur and minimising damage to fish stocks.

- Carrying out habitat improvements for the benefit of resident fish.

- Constructing fish passes to allow migratory fish like salmon and sea trout free passage upriver to their spawning grounds.

- Monitoring the increase or decline in fish numbers in various waters by analysing anglers' catch returns, juvenile fish surveys and fish counters.

- Acting on the results of these surveys by advising on the stocking of fish to restore or improve a fishery.

- Carrying out fisheries research to assist future improvements and developments.

Do all anglers drink like the proverbial?

FISH GET STUNG

In 2003 a team of researchers from the Roslin Institute and the University of Edinburgh injected bee venom and acetic acid into the lips of a number of trout while a separate control group of fish received a jab of saline. The researchers then observed that the fish that had been 'stung' on the lips tried to rub their mouths on the side of the tank, while the others carried on swimming placidly around in circles. From this the researchers drew the brilliant conclusion that fish feel pain. What they did not say is that while fish have an elaborate system of sensory cells around their mouths, they do not possess the necessary brainpower to register pain. According to a study by a Professor Rose of the University of Wyoming, fish do not have a neo-cortex in their brains – in other words, the main pain receptor of their grey matter isn't there.

FISHING FLIES NAMED AFTER WOMEN

Many flies used in trout or salmon fishing are named after women or appear to be connected with them in some way. For example, the 'Alexandra fly' is named after Princess Alexandra. Here are a few more:

1. Kate McLaren
2. Meg in her braws
3. Alexandra
4. Damsel nymph
5. Yellow Sally
6. Baby doll
7. Dogsbody
8. Golden Anna
9. Heather moth
10. Ladybird
11. Merry widow
12. Painted lady
13. Hairy Mary
14. Lady Caroline
15. Meg with the muckle mo'

QUOTE UNQUOTE

Anglers, unlike excisemen, have no grounds of complaint against the definition given of their occupation in Johnson's Dictionary.
WC Stewart, pioneering nineteenth-century Scottish angler

FEAR THE WEEVER

The weever is Britain's only poisonous fish and a decidedly nasty little piece of work. They are often caught by sea anglers fishing from the shore. Because they are diminutive greedy beasts averaging only six inches or so in length, the fish will often snaffle up bait meant for larger saltwater fish. Once impaled you will have the devil's own job getting them off the hook. The fish's dorsal fin has a row of venomous needles, which the little jerk tries very hard to stick through your fingers. The pain from being stabbed by the fins is quite intense and your hand will swell up for a while, which is not recommended for a happy day's fishing. You will immediately recognise this species by its stumpy head, stringy anal fin and dark brown back on which are displayed a neat range of hypodermics. Keep at arm's length and handle with very thick gloves or a long pair of surgical pliers.

Age in years at which esteemed angler Bernard Venables, creator of Mr Crabtree, the cult fishing figure of classic cartoons, died

A GREAT ESCAPE

The Hungarian escapologist Harry Houdini was renowned for extricating himself from strange situations. In the early 1900s a strange 'sea monster' possibly a large whale, was washed up on a beach at Boston, Massachusetts. This creature was embalmed for public view. Houdini took it upon himself to be handcuffed and was then forced through an opening in the side of the monster. The carcass was then sewn up and sealed with chains and Houdini left inside. Fifteen minutes later Houdini escaped and appeared at the monster's side. It is not known if he sustained his efforts with a little sushi.

A BIT FISHY

Which warm-blooded mammal shares its name with
both a type of fish and a type of fly?
Answer on page 153.

TERRIBLE FISHING JOKES

'I was fishing off the pier when, would you believe it, a little sand eel no bigger than my pinkie took the bait. Next a big cod came along and swallowed the sand eel but before I could get the cod reeled in a shark appeared and grabbed the cod.'

'Did you land the shark?'

'No, the bloody eel let go.'

MIND YOUR BAROMETRICS

A popular old wives' tale claims that trout will 'rise' – that is, they will be more inclined to feed and therefore be caught – on a 'rising glass' whereas a barometric glass which is falling might mean the fish go off in a deep sulk and refuse to bite. Not only that but it is said that fish are aware of a change in barometric pressure before it even happens. While this theory has found favour with anglers, especially if they are at a loss to explain the behaviour of their fickle quarry, scientists generally dismiss the idea, stating that fish underwater sense very little change in atmospheric pressure. Fish have unique swim bladders which allow them to pass easily through different depths of water, so a change in pressure in the air, the scientists say, makes little or no difference to their movements.

So if you're looking for an excuse for not catching any fish, you can cross that one off the list.

James Dubravius that Moravian, in his book de pisc telleth, how travelling by the highway side in Silesia, he found a nobleman, 'booted up to the groins' wading himself, pulling the nets, and labouring as much as any fisherman of them all: and when some belike objected to him the baseness of his office, he excused himself, 'that if other men might hunt hares, why should not he hunt carps?' Many gentlemen in like sort with us will wade up to the arm-holes upon such occasions, and voluntarily undertake that to satisfy their pleasure, which a poor man for a good stipend would scarce be hired to undergo. Plutarch, in his book de soler. Animal. Speaks against all fishing, 'as a filthy, base, illiberal employment, having neither wit nor perspicacity in it, nor worth the labour'. But he that shall consider the variety of baits for all seasons, and pretty devices which our anglers have invented, peculiar lines, false flies, several sleights, etc., will say, that it deserves like commendation, requires as much study and perspicacity as the rest, and is preferred before many of them. Because hawking and hunting are very laborious, much riding, and many dangers accompany them; but this is still and quiet: and if so be the angler catch no fish, yet he hath a wholesome walk to the brookside, pleasant shade by the sweet silver streams; he hath good air, and sweet smells of fine fresh meadow flowers, he hears the melodious harmony of birds, he sees the swans, herons, ducks, waterhorns, coots etc. and many other fowl, with their brood, which he thinketh better than the noise of the hounds, or blast of horns, and all the sport they can make'.

Robert Burton,
The Anatomy of Melancholy

ANGLERS YOU WON'T MIND MEETING ON THE RIVERBANK

The Apprentice

Apprentice anglers are furiously keen and absorb all things fishy like a sponge. They are usually the first to arrive at the water, though not always the last to leave. Normally they have little time for contemplative analysis. The rod will be up in a flash and the water whipped to a foam before you have even drawn breath. If they are very young, this angler may develop a more patient, thoughtful approach; however, should they be in their middle years, conversion to higher ground may be more difficult. Apprentices are unfortunately given to asking the same question again and again in slightly different ways and then not listening to the answer. They are instantly recognised by ear-splitting grins when things are going well, and slumped shoulders and fat lips when things are not.

REDS UNDER BEDS

Fish caught by anglers that have an association with the colour red:

Red drum – Also known as redfish or channel bass, this fish is found off the USA coast from Massachusetts to Mexico. They make delicious eating and are highly prized by anglers who consider them great sport.

Red fish – The red fish was an ancient name given to salmon by superstitious sea fisherman who considered them unlucky.

Red herrings – So called because the pungent preserving process rendered them red.

Red bellies – In the nineteenth century char were often referred to as red bellies owing to their reddish hue.

Red troots – In the eighteenth century Scottish brown trout were often known as 'red troots', perhaps because of their red flesh which made them good eating. How they made the transition from red to brown is lost in angling antiquity.

JUST KEEP SWIMMING

When designing a family or city coat of arms, the herald had often to incorporate a fish in the drawing. This could be done in four different ways. The fish could be 'endowed' that is swimming to the left (as seen by the viewer) with a distinct arched back. Alternatively it could be 'hauriant', which meant it was swimming vertically upwards. Failing that it could be 'naiant' which meant it was swimming in a straight line to the left as seen by the viewer or last but not least, the fish could be 'uriant', sometimes spelt 'urinant'. This last term meant swimming or diving vertically downwards.

AS FAST AS A FISH

Anglers have always considered the speed at which a fish travels through water an important factor in helping to determine fishing tactics. In the 1960s a Dr Bainbridge came up with a formula by which the speed of a fish could be calculated. It was $V = \frac{3}{4}(L \ (f - \frac{4}{3}))$ where V equals velocity per second, L equals total length of the fish and f (which must be greater than five) is the number of tail beats per second. For mathematically-minded anglers this must have been a great boon. However the formula had one serious drawback. The rate of tail beats and the length of the prospective fish had to be known in advance of the calculation and since anglers never really know what is going to latch on next to the end of their line the theory has not been widely used.

SUPERSTITIONS OF THE SEAFARERS

The Sabbath

Fishing on a Sunday in Scotland has long been a bone of legal contention among freshwater anglers. Historically, sea-going fishermen were of similar persuasion but for superstitious rather than legal reasons. In the 1800s some said it was lucky to put to sea on the Sabbath, notably those setting sail from Prestonpans. However, at Dunbar and Stonehaven, the herring fishery is said to have collapsed because the boats chose to set sail on a Sunday. Nowadays with so few fish left in the sea, fishermen not only do not fish on a Sunday but also have extra, enforced 'tie up' days.

MOST EXCITING FIGHTS ON THE RIVER

1. Play a plastic bag for half an hour in fast water.
2. Wrestle with a small bale of chicken wire, which trundles along on the bottom, in an oddly slow rotation.
3. Play a waterlogged dead sheep to a standstill.
4. Catch the push bar of a supermarket trolley.
5. Snag your lure in the laces of an old boot, size eight upwards for greatest excitement.
6. Snag your lure in the lace of an old boot still on a corpse.
7. Catch a fertiliser bag on one side near its neck so it opens and closes in the current, guaranteed to work you to exhaustion.

MAKING WADERS

The first waders to be used by anglers were little more than leather boots of various lengths, which, according to the old masters, afflicted the angler with cold feet, sciatica and rheumatism. However, with the invention of rubberised materials in the nineteenth century, anglers found they could wade for longer without suffering as many ailments. Unfortunately the first rubber boot waders were extremely heavy and stiff as a board, so what was gained in waterproofing was sadly lost in general comfort. Things improved from the 1950s when manufacturers got to grips with combining nylon and softer rubberised cloth materials. Suddenly wearing waders became more of a pleasure and less of an endurance test. Waterproof, 'breathable' materials are now commonly used in wader manufacture and these are a boon on a hot day; however, they have a higher tendency to leak at the seams than the old clumpy rubber boots. Swings and roundabouts.

FISHY BRITISH PLACE NAMES

1. Shadwell, London
2. Eel Pie Island
3. Laxford Bridge
3. Fishponds, Bristol
5. Ely
6. Loch Nam Breac
7. Skelly Nab
8. Laxey, Isle of Man
9. Fishguard
10. Fishbourne

A LITERARY CATCH

Another solitary man was fishing further along the canal, but Arthur knew that they would leave each other in peace, would not even call out greetings. No one bothered you: you were the hunter, a dreamer, your own boss, away from it all for a few hours on any day that the weather did not throw down its rain. Like the corporal in the army who said it was marvellous the things you thought about as you sat on the lavatory. Even better than that, it was marvellous the things that came to you in the tranquillity of fishing.

He drank tea from the flask and ate a cheese sandwich, then sat back to watch the red and white float – up to its waist in water under alder trees – and keep an eye always close to it for the sudden indication of a fortunate catch. For himself, his own catch had been made, and he would have to wrestle with it for the rest of his life. Whenever you caught a fish, the fish caught you, in a way of speaking, and it was the same with anything else you caught, like the measles or a woman. Everyone in the world was caught, somehow, one way or another, and those that weren't were always on the way to it. As soon as you were born you were captured by fresh air that you screamed against the minute you came out. Then you were roped in by a factory, had a machine slung around your neck, and then you were hooked up by the arse by a wife. Mostly you were like a fish: you swam about with freedom, thinking how good it was to be left alone, doing anything you wanted to do and caring about no one, when suddenly: SPLUTCH! – the big hook clapped itself into your mouth and you were caught. Without knowing what you were doing you had chewed off more than you could bite and had to stick with the same piece of bait for the rest of your life. It meant death for a fish, but for a man it might not be so bad.

Alan Silletoe, *Saturday Night and Sunday Morning*

FAMOUS ANGLERS WHO NEVER WERE

J R Hartley
A popular *Yellow Pages* advert featured an actor playing the part of an elderly gentleman who, having tried a few places in the directory, finally found a bookshop which stocked a tome that he had written, entitled *Fly Fishing* by J R Hartley. So realistic was the ad, that English angling writer Peter Lapsley ghostwrote a book of the same name and enjoyed moderate success with it.

Mr Crabtree
Beginning in 1947 the *Daily Mirror* carried a very successful cartoon-style column called *Mr Crabtree goes Fishing*. In it a wise elderly gent advises his young protégé Peter on the finer arts of fishing. Mr Crabtree did not exist, however, and was created by esteemed English angler Bernard Venables, who died in his ninety-fourth year in 2001.

Brad Pitt
In the film directed by Robert Redford *A River Runs through It,* the character played by Brad Pitt appears to be an expert caster and catcher of fish. In fact, most if not all his fly fishing sequences were ghosted by expert US anglers, including the great Jason Borger, who executed the famous 'shadow casting' sequence.

QUOTE UNQUOTE

Fishermen constitute a separate class or sub race among the inhabitants of the earth.
Grover Cleveland, twentieth-century American angler

LOVE AMADOU

Anglers are known for being adaptable people and when they could find nothing on which to dry their fishing flies, they resorted to an increasingly scarce fungus known as amadou. This is a dark golden fungus which grows on fallen birch trees, in an oddly bulging shape. Apparently it got its name from the French word amadou, meaning lover, although quite why the French called it that might have something to do either with its pouting lips profile – or the fact that it is easy to ignite. Among many other uses, it has been used as tinder, firework ignition and a material to stop dental bleeding. Its use in fly fishing reached a peak in the early twentieth century, but after two world wars the material became more and more difficult to source. Sadly nowadays amadou, like the good lover, has become increasingly hard to find.

Oh, oh, there's that bailiff again...

HOW NOT TO DESCRIBE YOUR FISHING ROD

The fishing world is full of double entendres, especially when you try and converse about rods. Here are a few examples of how not to discuss the merits of a rod, especially in mixed company:

1. 'Mine's bigger than yours.'
2. 'I like a stiff one.'
3. 'Does it extend any further?'
4. 'You've got a big butt there.'
5. 'It's got male-female spigots.'
6. 'Your butt's a bit slippery.'

KNOW YOUR OLIGOS FROM YOUR EUTROS

Oligotrophic is the name given to a water (normally a lake) that is relatively poor in dissolved nutrients. The term is derived from the Greek 'oligoi', which means 'few'. If you are fishing oligotrophic waters, of which there are many in the more mountainous areas of Britain, then you are likely to find that the fish are on the small side as they are unable to access any rich sources of food. A eutrophic water, on the other hand, con- tains heaps of dissolved chemical nutrients, which in turn encour- age a lush food supply for the resident fish species. Oligos are not without some charm, howev- er, usually being grand, deep affairs – Loch Rannoch in Scot- land is a prime example – and often they contain very large trout known as ferox. Ferox can attain weights in excess of 20lbs and, although tricky to fish for, they are considered a great prize for the dedicated game fisher.

England's elegant dries

While their fishing neighbours adopted practical approaches to their fishing, the English for a time allowed themselves to be swept away in a tidal wave of fishing fashion. When the dry fly, a fly that floats on the water surface rather than sinking below it, was first popularised in the late nineteenth century, England's fishing glitterati deemed it to be the height of angling elegance. For a time any other method was frowned upon, if not banned altogether. Gentlemen of the Shires used 'dray flay', ruffians and rogues did not. Yes, it was that silly. As with many trends in social snobbery, it took two world wars to put the fashion of the immaculately dressed mayfly back in perspective.

MAKE MINE A DOUBLE

You might think that the cry, 'Make mine a double', is associated only with the consumption of whisky, but it also has a strong connection with fishing. 'The wee double' or 'double hook' has been around since the seventeenth century and is supposed to make doubly sure that your catch does not fall off. Fish with soft mouths taking the fly or baited hook might only do so lightly, but the fact that there are two hooks there rather than one is said to ensure capture. The English tend to call this two-hook ploy the 'double iron or 'double hook' while the Scots call it a 'wee double'. The 'wee' part is apparently derived from the old Scots word 'wei', which meant a 'bit of a thing'. It later became associated with something small, but can actually mean the opposite – for example, 'Let's have a wee dram', usually means that a long night of imbibing is ahead.

THE SECRET OF THE SHOAL

Going into a vast swirling shoal is the little fish's secret weapon against larger predators. Those underwater films of oceanic fish rising and falling in great columns, circles and twists are not staged for the camera. However hypnotically beautiful the shoals may be, the fish are swimming like that with only one objective in mind – self preservation. Apparently, bigger predators are confused by the brilliant flashing silver clouds initiated by the little darting fish as they switch directions with lightning speed. Interestingly, the fish at the centre of the shoal are not necessarily the safest. Predators befuddled by the flickering fishy lights in front of them tend to bludgeon into the core of the shoal with mouths wide open and it's a swift end for those unlucky enough to be in the middle at the time.

QUOTE UNQUOTE

It's shocking that people will still go fishing for fun.
Dawn Carr, People for the Ethical Treatment of Animals (PETA)

GAME TACKLE

Sometimes you will meet a fly fisher by the river, who appears to be weighed down with the fishing accoutrements dangling about his person. These are likely to include:

A zillion boxes of flies for every occasion
Spare spools
A landing net
Nylon with droppers
Nylon without droppers
Zingers
Gink bottles (makes flies float)
Zink bottles (makes them sink)
Line tray
Fluorocarbon
Nippers
Fly patches

A BIT FISHY

Which 1960s wild man of rock retired to run
a trout fishery in England?
Answer on page 153.

A RISE OR TWO

When a trout is said to be 'rising', that means that it is coming up to the surface of the water, taking a food item, and then heading back down to the depths. During the actual 'rise', a movement of some sort will be seen in the water. Fishermen set great store by these types of rise forms, as they are said to indicate what the trout is feeding on and therefore what fly the angler should use to imitate the insect that will catch the fish.

Rise forms are anything from a slash rise, which occurs when the trout is chasing down a fast-moving insect, to a head and tail rise, which means the fish could perhaps be feeding on insect pupae. Sometimes the fish makes a sort of whorl in the water, in which case it is a 'boil' rise. Every now and then the feeding trout just makes little more than a gentle sip, which is known as the 'kiss' rise. The origin of the 'trout pout', perhaps.

Most weekends, starting in the spring
Until late summer, I spend angling.
Not for fish. I find that far too tame
But for birds, a much more interesting game.

A juicy worm I use as bait
Cast a line into the tree and wait
Seldom for long (that's half the fun)
A commotion in the leaves, the jobs half done.

Pull hard, jerk home the hook
Then reel him in. Let's have a look
A tiny thing, a fledgling, young enough to spare.
I show mercy. Unhook, and toss it to the air.

It flies nestwards and disappears among the leaves
(What man roasts and braises, he too reprieves)
What next? A magpie. Note the splendid tail.
I wring its neck. Though stringy it'll pass for quail.

Unlike water, the depths of trees are high
So, standing back, I cast into the sky.
And ledger there beyond the topmost bough,
Until threshing down, like a black cape, screams a crow!

Evil creature! A witch in feathered form.
I try to net the dark, encircling storm.
It caws for help. Its cronies gather round
They curse and swoop. I hold my ground.

An infernal mass, a black, horrific army
I'll not succumb to Satan's origami.
I reach into my coat, I've come prepared,
Bring out my pocket scarecrow – Watch out bird!

Its cross shaped, the sign the godless fear
In a thunderflap of wings they disappear.
Except of course, that one, ungainly kite
Broken now, and quickly losing height.

I haul it in, and with a single blow
Dispatch it to that Aviary below.
The ebb and flow: magpie, thrush,
Nightingale and crow.
The wood darkens. Time to go.
I pack away the food I've caught

And thankful for a good day's sport
Amble home. The forest fisherman.
And I'll return as soon as I can

To bird. For I'm a birderer. The birderman.

Roger McGough,
The Birderman

FISH-LIKE SNAKES

*The most primitive types of fish are those
that resemble snakes. These include:*

The lamprey – With an appearance only a mother could love, this eel-like creature has a mouth like a funnel ringed inside with knife-like teeth. Its main aim in life is to suck the lifeblood from its other unsuspecting fishy brethren. Sea and river lampreys are wretched parasites, particularly of salmon; the smaller brook lamprey does not do quite as much damage. Happily the tables have turned on this big sucker, as it is now a popular means of baiting the hook for other predatory species like pike.

The freshwater eel – Eels are probably the most misunderstood of all fish species. Their most unusual feature is an ability to travel huge distances by water and by wriggling overland. No other fish has this unique ability to swim on land and sea. Not only that, but every eel migrates all the way to the Sargasso Sea to spawn, unfailingly year after year, an immense journey for such a small creature. They are common across all of Britain and most of Europe and despite their slimy wriggly appearance they have been highly prized as a food source over many centuries.

The garfish – A sea-dwelling species which, from a distance, looks like a two-foot-long green snake with a pronounced thin snout. This beak is employed rather like a truncheon and the fish uses it to knock out its prey before swallowing them. Sea anglers say you will know when one is about to be hooked, as there is a strange but distinct tap tap on the line quite unlike most other fish.

The oarfish – Growing up to four metres long, the oarfish is the longest bony fish in the sea. These are probably the creatures responsible for the sea serpent legends perpetuated by ancient mariners. Despite its fearsome appearance the oarfish is a harmless creature feeding mainly on a diet of plankton. They are very occasionally pulled up by some shocked and surprised anglers off the British coastline, but this is a rare occurrence.

ANGLERS YOU MIGHT WANT TO AVOID

The Local Expert

Local Experts talk incessantly about themselves and their latest successes, engaging you in a weird sort of continuous loop of conversation into which you fail to insert a word. They are easily recognised by their flushed and seriously smug faces when fish have been caught. However, if they have not bagged anything, they instantly vanish so as to avoid the post-match analysis in the pub. Irritatingly their knowledge is often good for their local patch but take heart in the fact that it can fluctuate wildly if they fish unfamiliar territory. Often Local Experts team up with less experienced fishers who, sadly, pander to the Expert's inflated sense of self-worth.

FISH ARTISTS

Drawing fish isn't easy. Here are a few modern artists who make it look effortless:

Robin Ade

Robin Armstrong

Paul Cook

Neil Dalrymple

David Hughes

Charles Jardine

Terence Lambert

Mick Loates

Rodger McPhail

Richard Smith

BRITANNIA'S JAWS?

In early 2005, the *Daily Mail* reported that a disproportionately high number of dead porpoises had been washed up on the British coastline between the Scottish borders and North Lincolnshire. Marine experts said that bite marks on the unfortunate porpoises indicated a predatory shark was on the loose, most likely a shortfin mako, a species more commonly found in Asiatic waters. Global warming was apparently to blame for this unusual fish's presence, as warmer sea temperatures have allowed it to roam further afield than is the norm. However, even if the killer had turned out to be a mako shark, we would have to forgive and forget, as this fish is the tenth most endangered species in the world. In the meantime coastal fishermen were warned to beware of anything with snapping jaws and big teeth appearing in their nets.

Weight, in ounces, of a record-breaking freshwater eel caught on the St Croix River Minnesota in the 1980s

BRING ON THE PICTURES

It might surprise you to know that, despite the centuries-old abiding interest anglers have had in making artificial flies to copy natural insects, nobody ever thought of producing an illustrated guide, which linked the real fly directly to its hand-made imitation. It was not until the mid nineteenth century that an angler eventually twigged that it might be a good idea to give anglers some pictorial guidance in this department. In 1836 one Alfred Ronalds produced *The Flyfishers Entomology*, which did just that, identifying and illustrating a string of creepy crawlies and buzzing flies and giving the dressing of an imitation beside it. Before Ronalds' incredibly simple yet effective book, fishermen had to more or less guess at what fly should be used to copy a particular fluttery bug. The fact that Ronalds' book was reprinted several times and sold well for over a century just shows that to an angler, a picture can be worth a thousand words.

FISH WE SHOULD EAT

According to the Marine Conservation Society there are certain species of fish that we should eat in the name of conservation. These fish come from well-managed sustainable stocks and include:

Black bream • Cape hake • Cuttlefish
Dover sole • Flounder • Herring
Mackerel • Megrim • Pacific cod
Pacific salmon • Red gurnard
Whiting • Witch

SOMETHING IN THE WATER

Male fish species are coming under increasing threat from the amounts of hormone-altering substances being found in groundwater and watercourses throughout the UK. While it might be thought that this is putting fish in touch with their feminine side, in the long term there could be such a major reduction of productivity in various fish species, and fragile fish populations could become extinct. It seems the fish are absorbing endocrine disruptors, which come from, among other sources, pesticides, plasticisers, PCBs and synthetic and natural oestrogens. As a consequence of this insidious and ever-present pollution, male fish are becoming feminised.

The male gudgeon, for example, has been particularly hard hit, with eggs appearing in the testes. It has not taken to cross-dressing as yet.

A LITERARY CATCH

I had different ways of occupying myself while I lay awake. I would think of a trout stream I had fished along when I was a boy and fish its whole length very carefully in my mind; fishing very carefully under all the logs, all the turns of the bank, the deep holes and the clear shallow stretches, sometimes catching trout and sometimes losing them. I would stop fishing at noon to eat my lunch; sometimes on a log over the stream; sometimes on a high bank under a tree, and I always ate my lunch very slowly and watched the steam below me while I ate. Often I ran out of bait because I would take only ten worms with me in a tobacco tin when I started. When I had used them all I had to find more worms, and sometimes it was very difficult digging in the bank of the stream where the cedar trees kept out the sun and there was no grass but only the bare moist earth and often I could find no worms. Always though I found some kind of bait, but one time in the swamp I could find no bait at all and had to cut up one of the trout I had caught and use him for bait.

Ernest Hemingway, *Now I Lay Me*

USELESS TACKLE

1. A waterproof jacket that leaks after only a micro split
2. Nylon stored in bright sunlight
3. Collapsible landing nets in need of Viagra
4. A reel full of grit
5. Hats that blow off
6. Breathable waders designed to take osmosis seriously

SCRUMPTIOUS BASS

Sea bass are now recognised as one of the UK's best eating fish. The fish command a high price around the country and are the height of gourmet fashion. Sea anglers lucky enough to catch one should bear in mind they can only take it home if it's over 41 centimetres long. They must also remember that there are special designated Bass Nursery Protection Areas (34) off the UK coast and fishing by boat there, for bass, will not be allowed.

Once you've landed your legal catch, take it home with pride, gut carefully, for the spines are hypodermics, and season the gut cavity with salt and a little white pepper. Score the thick skin and rub in some garlic and parsley butter. Grill gently until the flesh whitens. Eat with relish and a morsel of samphire if you have it near; if not, a little rocket salad and new minted potatoes does the trick. Top off with a good pinot grigio.

HOW FISH GOT THEIR NAMES

Salmon

During the eighth century, salmon were known in Old English as 'leax'. This term has survived across Britain in place names like Laxford Bridge in northern Scotland, Leixlip (meaning salmon leap) in Ireland and Laxey, Isle of Man. Post Norman Invasion the Old French term 'saumon' became absorbed into the English language via a corruption with the Latin name *Salmo salar*. By the 1300s the name salmon was in common use and has remained with us ever since. Variously salmon are also referred to as the 'King of Fish', 'Salar the Leaper' and in Scotland anglers will speak of 'taking a fish from the pool'. The 'fish' in question is always a salmon, all other fish species like trout or perch will be referred to by their appropriate names.

QUOTE UNQUOTE

Fishing is not just a matter of life or death,
it is far more important than that.
Origin unknown, also applied to football and golf

FISH ARE SUPERIOR BEINGS

According to a recent issue of the periodical *Fish & Fisheries*, fish are 'steeped in social intelligence, pursue Machiavellian strategies of manipulation, punishment and reconciliation... exhibit stable cultural traditions and co-operate to inspect predators and catch food'. While this is comforting to know, the Irish have been au fait with the 'fish are smart' concept for years. In Irish mythology, Fionn MacCumhaill was bestowed with superhuman powers when he caught and ate salmon. This fish was called the 'salmon of knowledge'. Nothing new in the sea then.

CROSS-DRESSING CUTTLEFISH

Apparently there are four male giant Australian cuttlefish to every one of the female of the species. This means the male fish have to resort to some subterfuge in order to attract a mate. This they do by disguising their male characteristics and changing their colour in order to resemble the female's mottled appearance. The already paired resident female and male cuttlefish are tricked into believing it's just another lady in their midst. Sneakily when the resident male has its back turned the incoming cross-dresser dashes in and mates with the female. Who said fish are dumb!

Now I know what the fish feel like.

FAMOUS LADIES IN FISHING

HM Queen Elizabeth the Queen Mother

The late Queen Mother was a highly skilled salmon fisher, frequently casting flies on Scottish waters including the Thurso near her beloved retreat the Castle of Mey in Caithness and the River Dee at Balmoral. By the time she was in her mid 20s her expertise with a salmon rod was already legendary. After the tragic loss of her husband the King, she found some solace in angling, and few could match her doubty determination to catch fish in all weathers, which she did so frequently.

A PINCH OF CARP

Carp in the UK have now become such a designer fishing item that they attract the unwarranted attentions of specialist thieves. Big fish are being stolen almost to order, as resale on the black market can net the unscrupulous a very tidy sum. Large carp of 25lb and upward are quite rare in England and can now command prices of thousands, rather than hundreds, of pounds sterling. The English Environment Agency has advised lake owners to take photographs of their prize fish so that they can be identified later if they ever resurface in someone else's pond. A case of, could all carp smile please, for their own safety.

Weight, in pounds, of the third-placed world record Nile perch caught on Lake Nasser in 2002. First place was 179 pounds and second 120 pounds

WHAT TO DO WITH THE FISH

Smoke it • Poach it
Pickle it • Salt it
Grill it • Fry it
Bake it • Barbecue it
Steam it • Souse it

THE OTTER – FRIEND OR FOE

The otter and the angler have had a strange on-off love affair over the centuries. As far back as 600AD fishermen have used otters to help them catch fish. During the Tang Dynasty, fishermen reared wild otters by hand with the aim of getting them to help their fishing efforts. The otters were so well trained they would, on command, swim out and drive unsuspecting shoals of fish towards the waiting nets. The otters effectively did the legwork in return for a few fish from the main catch. This practice continued in China until the beginning of the twentieth century. In Europe similar tales are told of otters being trained to 'round up' fish for the fishermen's nets. In Sweden there are sixteenth century records of otters being trained to collect fish from small stock ponds and bring them to the cook of the house, who would presumably reward the otter with some scraps.

Comparable tales of this symbiotic relationship continued in England until around the nineteenth century, when suddenly the otter took on a completely different mantle and became regarded as the angler's foe rather than his friend. Gamekeepers on Victorian sporting estates took to hunting, trapping or shooting otters as they insisted that they were taking too many valuable fish from the rivers. Otter populations dramatically diminished and it was not until the 1950s that otter hunting finally came to a halt. Scientific evidence finally proved that the wild otter fed more on eels in freshwater and crustaceans while at sea. And although they were partial to game fish, they did not do the huge amount of damage that the old gamekeepers had alleged.

While the wild otter has been accepted back into angling circles, there is a peculiar irony in the fact that one of the most lethal devices in fish poaching is called the 'otter'. This is a plank of wood with a string of baited hooks beneath it, which is roped up and then floated out into river or lake and left to bob about while fish impale themselves on the hooks. The poacher then returns (usually in the dead of night), pulls in the rope and the 'otter' obligingly brings in the catch. A cold-blooded rather than warm-blooded fishing friend...

Banquet Given in 1466. The Great Feast at the intronization of the reverende father in God George Nevell, Archbishop of York, and Chauncelour of Englande in the sixth yere of the raigne of kyng Edwarde the fourth.

And first the goodly provision made for the same.

Here foloweth the serving of fishe in order.

The First Course

First potage, Almonde butter, Red Herrynges, Salt fysch, Luce salt, Ele, Kelyng, Codlyng, and Hadocke boyled, Thirlepoole rost. Pyke in Rarblet, Eeles baked, Samon chynes broiled, Turbut baked, And Fritters fryed.

The Seconde Course

Freshe Samon jowls, salt Sturgion, Whytynges, Pylchers, Eeles, Makerels, Places fryed, Barbelles, Conger rost, Troute, Lamprey rost, Bret, Turbut, Roches, Samon baked, Lynge in gelly, Breame baked, Tenche in gelly, Crabbes.

The Third Course

Jowles of fresh Sturgion, Great Eels, Broyled Conger, Cheuens, Breames, Rudes, Lamprones, Small Perches fryed, Smeltes rost, Shrympes, Small Menewes, Thirlpool baked and Lopster.

John Leland, *De Rebus Britannicis Collectanea*, Volume VI

A BIT FISHY

For what fishing exploit is the Roman Aelian
of the third century AD famous?
Answer on page 153.

GOLDFISH STRIKES IT LUCKY

Following floods engulfing the town of Carlisle in January 2005, two goldfish were rescued from the local football ground as the water was being pumped from the pitch. One of the fish was recognised as 'Judy', a local pet refugee who had been carried away in the floods. Judy's owner has agreed the fish can be adopted as the club mascot for the Carlisle United team. The lucky goldfish will be cared for by the daughter of the club owner who had pluckily saved the fish from being hoovered back up in the floodwater. When Judy is not on official mascot duty the second fish, as yet unnamed, will act as substitute.

*Go fishing for your solace, to procure the health
of your body and especially your soul.*
Dame J Berners, in The *Treatise of Fishing with an Angle*

DAMMED IF I DO

Imagine you are a fish for a moment. There you are swimming away quite happily knowing your own limits, where the lake world begins and ends. Suddenly this great whoosh of water comes in and before you know it, there you are feeding in a field! For a while, life is just rosy. All those juicy worms and snails you could never get at before are now right there in front of you. You eat better than you have done in years and grow sleek and fat. But after the feast, the famine arrives. All the extra food disappears, washed away in waves twice as big as they ever were before. And the lake has something weird about it. Your world is not the same. The water goes up and down alarmingly especially when some gigantic gate opens at one end and everything gets sucked out.

Welcome to your new life in the reservoir.

NET THE CATCH

Fishermen worldwide use a variety of different
nets to land their catch. These include:

Bag nets • Gill nets • Haaf nets
Herry-water nets • Ladle nets
Landing nets • Net and cobble
Poke nets • Seine nets • Shoulder nets
Stake nets • Stoop nets • Triangle nets
Whammel nets • Yair nets

DRINK TO YOUR HEALTH

Famous for rice wine they may be, but it seems the Chinese have now turned their attentions to making wine from fish. In early 2005 the official Xinhua news agency reported that locals have developed a special brewery which 'will clean, boil and ferment fish for making wine' and that the wine produced 'is nutritious and contains low alcohol'. Entrepreneur Sun Keman has developed the 'Dalian Fisherman's Song Maritime Biological Brewery' and has already received orders from Russia and Japan, as well as other parts of China. Given China's thousands of years of expertise in brewing procedures the result may be said to be waited upon with bated – or baited – breath.

ANGLING WORTH MORE THAN GOLF

According to a survey undertaken by Caledonian University in 2003 on behalf of the Scottish Executive, the sport of fishing in Scotland is worth one heck of a lot of cash. So much so that it puts golf well in the shade regarding the annual income it generates. The survey looked at data collected from visiting anglers, trade organisations, fisheries and river and loch riparian owners. After many computations, ruminations and extrapolations, the researchers came up with the statement that anglers spend a total of £113 million on angling in Scotland, with salmon anglers accounting for over 65% of this grand total. This beats golf income by some £1 million, if not more.

Fishing widows might be pleased to learn their better halves are contributing so much to the good of the economy.

THE IDEAL ANGLER SHOULD...

1. Be magnanimous; accept that failure is quite common.
2. Realise that angling is a lifelong learning experience to be savoured and worked on.
3. Learn from their mistakes.
4. Share accumulated knowledge and experiences with others, especially youngsters who are the life blood of the sport. You will get back more than you give out.
5. Get involved and be informed in matters of fish conservation, both in the practical and the scientific.
6. Treat fishing as a big adventure not an endurance test.

A RING OF TRUTH

One of the strangest catches of 2005 has to be a sailfish caught off the coast of Florida with a wedding ring round its nose. Not only that but the angler Eric Bartos who caught it knew just how it got there. Two years previously, he had symbolically slipped it on the fish's beak and returned it to the sea. He did so to symbolise the break up of his marriage, his lost love and the fact that he felt his love for fishing was at that time stronger. This time Bartos retrieved the wedding ring and gently released the fish back to the water.

Upon returning to shore few would believe this weird coincidence but after taking a lie detector test, Bartos's fishy tale does indeed appear to be true. His story so impressed his ex-wife she contacted him after over two years of silence and told him it might be a sign to 'make peace'.

ANGLERS YOU WON'T MIND MEETING ON THE RIVERBANK

The Duffer

Duffers are generally very amiable fishers usually in their mid to late years and it has to be said that an awful lot of anglers fall into this affable category. They catch a few fish but never seem particularly bothered about the need for consistent success. Habits include spending an inordinate amount of time in setting up tackle and then dropping bits of it particularly spectacles, scissors and small bottles of goo. Often they are quite knowledgeable, if they can remember what they are talking about. Sometimes they simply make it up as they go along, but they are always pleasant enough company.

YOU CAN TELL IT'S A FISH BY ITS...

Adipose fin
Caudal (fin)
Dorsal (fin)
Gills
Lateral line
Maxilla
Palatine teeth
Parr marks
Swim bladder
Vent

A LITERARY CATCH

Here the earth is fluid to my thought – the sky is reflected from beneath – and around yonder cape is highway to other continents. This current allies me to the world. Be careful to sit in an elevating and inspiring place. – There my thoughts were confined and trivial and I hid myself from the gaze of travellers. – Here they are expanded and elevated and I am charmed by the beautiful river reach. It is equal to a different season and country and creates a different mood.

As you travel northward from Concord – probably the reaches of the Merrimack River – looking up and down them from the bank – will be the first inspiring sight. There is something in the scenery of a broad river equivalent to culture and civilisation. – Its channel conducts our thoughts as well as bodies to classic and famous ports and allies us to all that is fair and great.

HD Thoreau, *Journal no 26*,
4 June to 8 July 1858

Who were the Rebeccaites?
Answer on page 153.

OLD PISCATORIALS – NEW EDITORIALS

A gal's best friend is her gillie.

QUOTE UNQUOTE

Old Fishermen don't die – they just smell that way.
Anon

FOODY FLIES

Bangers

Much as fish might like to munch on bangers and mash, these Bangers are specially designed flies which originate from the American saltwater fly stable. Bangers are closely related to flies known as 'poppers', which are brightly coloured flies shaped rather like a small stunted fish complete with big eyes. The blunted nose at the head of the fly makes both a considerable disturbance on the water surface and a strange popping sound, hence the name. Fish like the American wide-mouthed bass and some sea species like bonefish chase after the lure with gusto. In recent years British anglers have taken to using the fly for pike and rainbow trout with some success.

GERR 'ORFE

Though orfe are eaten in both Russia and Finland where they are commercially reared as farmed fish, the Brits are none too keen on them as a foodstuff, and instead either fish for them or keep them as pets in little ponds. The orfe (also known as the ide) is a spanking little fish reminiscent of a silvery goldfish, but larger. It comes in other colours notably blue or gold. These are non-native fish and were first introduced to Britain from Germany in the latter half of the nineteenth century. The fish were taken first to stock the lakes and ponds of Woburn Abbey, but further introductions have seen orfe spread across the UK, for both ornamental and sporting use. Coarse anglers generally rate them highly and the popularity of orfe fishing is on the up in the UK.

BEASTLY POACHING

Poaching of freshwater fish has been around ever since man discovered he could make money from selling the catch without paying to fish for it. For centuries the salmon has fallen foul of poaching. Here are a few examples of particularly nasty methods:

1. Leistering
2. Ottering
3. Netting
4. Sniggling
5. Worming
6. Prawning
7. Dragging
8. Burning
9. Cyaniding
10. Dynamiting

FIRST FIND YOUR RAM

The 'tup's indispensable' is the name famous angler GEM Skues gave to a well known highly successful trout fly tied originally by RS Austin in 1900. The secret ingredient in this pattern was the material used in the construction of its body. This 'dubbing', as it is known, was wool fibres but any old wool would not do – it had to be taken from ram's testicles. Austin kept the nature of this dusty yellow material a secret, and even when he died in 1914 the family maintained the mystery for a further 20 years, so as to have a monopoly on the supply of this 'rare' material to fly dressers. Modern fly tyers normally use substitutes like mohair or tinted knitting wool, and rams everywhere have heaved a sigh of relief.

TAKE ONE SWIM FEEDER

The main role of the coarse fisher's swim feeder is to liven up the fish in front of him. This it does by being cast out full of bait, such as maggots or special mixes, which then slowly disperses through the current, attracting fish to feed from far and wide, which the angler then tries to catch with rod and line. Like so much in fishing tackle today, there is a considerable variety of these secret weapons, including:

Block end feeders
Early method feeders
Fatal Attractors
Fox feeders
Maggot feeders
Method feeders
Oblong feeders
Open-ended feeders
Round feeders
Spods

A LITERARY CATCH

Eels are not produced from sexual intercourse, nor are they oviparous, nor have they been detected with semen or ova, nor when dissected do they appear to possess either seminal or uterine viscera; and this is the only kind of sanguineous animal which does not originate either in sexual intercourse or in ova. It is, however, manifest that this is the case, for, after rain, they have been reproduced in some marshy ponds, from which all the water was drawn and the mud cleaned out; but they are never produced in dry places nor in ponds that are always full, for they live upon and are nourished by rain water. It is plain, therefore, that they are not produced either from sexual intercourse or from ova. Some persons have thought that they were productive, because some eels have parasitic worms, and they thought these became eels.

This however, is not the case, but they originate in what are called the entrails of the earth, which are found spontaneously in mud and moist earth. The have been observed making their escape from them, and others have been found in them when cut up and dissected. These originate both in the sea and in rivers wherein putrid matter is abundant: in those places in the sea which are full of fuci (seaweeds) and near the banks of rivers and ponds, for in these places the heat causes much putridity. This is the mode of generation in eels.

Aristotle, *Historia Animalium* **Book VI, chapter xv**

Mayflies in flight look like angels.
Caddis flies look like moths on speed.
John Gierach, famous modern American angler and writer

A TALE OF VOE

Shetland is not perhaps the first place you would think of as a famous fishing destination. A trip to the Hampshire chalk-streams maybe, but a long troop involving rough sea crossings and overnighters all the way to windblown Shetland?

What on earth for? But although Shetland is more or less forgotten now as a fishing destination, early twentieth-century anglers went there in droves. Their quarry was the large sea trout, which were then prolific along Shetland's indented coastline. Although saltwater fishing on the islands never quite achieved the cult status of 1930s big game tunny fishing off Scarborough, a considerable number of the great and good braved the long trip to these islands. Not for nothing did northern men of the cloth hold group meetings on Shetland during July and August, the peak times for sea trout fishing. Local legend has it that they would time their devotions so that they could stop and high-tail it down to the shore to fish for the big trout coming in on the turn of the tide.

Anglers fished predominantly in sea 'voes', a word that comes from ancient Norse meaning a firth, bay or creek. The fishers would position themselves in these long rocky inlets so that the fish would have to pass them by as they headed up on the incoming tide toward the freshwater river at the head of the voe. The sea trout ran up and spawned in these freshwater burns in October, but for the rest of the year they would mooch around the Shetland coastline, feeding on the rich diet of crustaceans and sand eels. Thus the incoming tide would bring a shoal of sea trout into the voe and angling timing was critical. The fish did not stay long, just long enough to nose the waters of their natal stream before scooting seaward again, so it was up to the angler to be in the right place at the right time.

Sadly the sea trout fishing reached a nadir in the late 1960s, when for some inexplicable reason the numbers of sea trout started to fall and, unsurprisingly, the number of wealthy anglers coming to Shetland correspondingly dropped off. Come the 1980s and the advent of fish farming, the wild sea trout numbers further declined and today Shetland fly fishers have largely left the voes to concentrate on the islands excellent freshwater lochs. Which is another little piece of British angling history gone west.

HAIR WINGS

It is thought that the originator of flies made with hair, as opposed to filaments from feather wings, was a rancher from Idaho. Apparently in the 1890s he took to dressing his fishing flies with tufts of bucktail. While the rest of Europe was at that time intent on making ever more delicate flies of fur and exotic feather, the Americans would have no such pretensions and persisted with incorporating hair into the fly body and wings. Apart from bucktail, their fly tyers also took to using bear, squirrel, coyote, deer and wood chuck hair in their creations. This across-the-pond split in fly tying skills persisted until about the 1980s, when the Brits finally absorbed some of the American novelties into their fly boxes – and they caught just as many fish.

SUPERSTITIONS OF THE SEAFARERS

Pass the salt

In Scotland, superstition has it that salt must never be mentioned while at sea. To do so was thought to bring immediate bad luck upon the fishing boat and its crew. There is a story from 1905 of an Eyemouth boat which ran short of salt while out trawling. The skipper hailed a Yarmouth drifter with the words: 'We need something we dinna want to speak aboot'. The English skip shouted back 'Is it salt ye want?' to which the Scot replied indeed it was and the precious commodity was handed over without mentioning it by name. The Scottish crew escaped certain doom by keeping below decks out of earshot while the discussion was going on.

WHAT SALMON – AGAIN!

Legend has it that in the seventeenth and eighteenth centuries the indentures of apprentices contained a clause stating that salmon was not to be served to them on more than two or three occasions per week. While this was a lovely tale, it was subsequently proven that no such exact clause existed. In 1955 a Mr Cohen wrote a paper called Apprentices and Salmon in the *Transactions of the Woolhope Naturalists Field Club Hertfordshire* (Vol XXXV, part 1), which discovered that poorly paid farm workers insisted on a diet of salmon being limited to just a few days per week, but dispelled the myth of the apprentice indenture clause.

Whatever the truth, it just goes to show how prolific salmon were in British rivers in the past. And now it is on the Protected Species list – changed days indeed.

'WE SHALL FIGHT THEM ON THE BEACHES'

It is said that Winston Churchill got the idea for what was to become one of his most rousing speeches in 1938 while cod fishing on a cold winter's day on a beach at Dungeness. Churchill was not only a keen sea angler, but also gained much inspiration from the simple pleasures of coarse fishing. The smoking room at Blenheim Palace once carried photographs of Churchill and Field Marshall Montgomery doing battle, not with the dogs of war, but with small rudd on English rivers like the Avon or Kennet. Here they would stretch out their roach poles, don their old leather bait aprons, launch a fine mix of ground bait (casters and hemp were favourites), catch innumerable small fishes, chew on a few fine cigars and almost certainly muse on the dramatic world events unfolding around them.

CASTING A LINE

If you thought fly fishing was simply standing up and waving a stick with a line attached, think again. These are just some of the types of fly line available today:

Double taper • Fast sink
Floating • Ghost tip
Hi Vis (high visibility)
Intermediate • Multi tips
Sink tip • Sinking
Shooting head
Spey lines • Slow sink
Twin-lines • Weight forward
Wetcel's

TOO MUCH OF A GOOD THING

Many non-anglers forget that, while fish like a bit of shade to give them cover from predators, too much of a good thing has the opposite effect and our finny friends do not flourish. In 2005, the River Yealm in Devon had got so overgrown with non native laurel bushes that the Environment Agency decided to put their laudable Salmon Action Plan into operation. This involved a team armed with axe and buzz saw removing several tonnes of dense leafy cover and thinning out the canopy sufficiently for light to penetrate the dark pools once more. This was intended to increase the biodiversity of all aquatic species and, it is hoped, to raise salmon survival rates by giving them back their natural range of food sources.

FISH WE SHOULD AVOID EATING

According to the Marine Conservation Society the list of fish below are taken from unsustainable, badly managed fisheries, which are already severely overfished. In the interests of long-term conservation, the fish we should avoid eating include:

- American plaice
- Atlantic cod (from overfished stocks)
- Atlantic halibut
- Atlantic salmon (wild)
- Chilean sea bass
- Grey mullet
- Grouper
- Ling
- Marlin (blue, Indo Pacific and white)
- Patagonian Toothfish (sea bass)
- Rays
- Shark
- Skates
- Snapper
- Sturgeon
- Swordfish
- Turbot (from the North Sea)

QUOTE UNQUOTE

I know what a shark looks like because I've seen one up close.
Chief Brody, *Jaws Two*

LETS GET FINNY

Despite being apparently small appendages, fins are terribly important to the survival of a fish. Quite simply, few fish species (apart from eels) can do without them, for they are needed to propel the fish along, help the fish keep their balance in a current and either speed up or slow the fish down. Two pectoral fins help to stabilise the fish and to change the direction in which it swims. The two pelvic fins and the one anal fin help the fish to rise and fall in the water while the dorsal and caudal (tail) fin act both as rudders and as the main means of propulsion. Though the classifications are seldom used now, fish can be divided into groups by the nature of their fins. 'Acanthopterygians' from the Greek akantha meaning thorn and 'pterugion' meaning wing are fish with spiny rays such as bass, perch or zander. 'Malacopterygians' from the Greek word malakos meaning soft are soft finned fishes like herring, trout or pike.

I NAME THIS TROUT

The trout of the Northern Hemisphere all come under the genus *Salmo trutta* yet have a huge range of names. Here are but a few;

Black finned trout • Brook trout • Brownies
Bull trout • Ferox • Finnock • Gillaroo
Golden trout • Sewin • Slob trout
Sonaghen • White trout

A LITERARY CATCH

'There's...' puff, puff, 'there's... puff, puff, 'A DEAD MAN IN THE RIVER!' my sister shouted. My mouth fell open, my boredom instantly gone. Jane was sweaty and pale and seemed to be trembling, although I couldn't tell if it was from the shock of seeing a dead man or from running up the hill so fast. There was a long, long silence while the two women stared down at her.

'What did you say?' Aunt Martha began. My sister was taking a deep breath, preparing to blurt out the information again, when our Aunt Madie intervened, stepping forward and grabbing Jane by the shoulders. She bent down and looked my sister in the face.

'You,' she said angrily, 'are lying!' and shook my sister. 'You're lying! Shame on you!'

'Noooo!' was all my sister could get out to the daunting figure in the black and white habit.

'Sister,' Aunt Martha offered hesitantly, 'I think she's telling the truth. Aren't you, Janie?'

I could not get off that stool or speak a word to help my sister. It was as though the heat had melted the seat of my shorts and a good portion of my butt to the wood and dried up my tongue. By now, my sister was badly frightened, and all I could do was watch Aunt Madie continue to shake the daylights out of Jane while Aunt Martha hovered around them in a nervous but ineffective spiral. Then Edgar Schroeder from Schroeder's Hardware Store across the street (and who I thought looked remarkably like Uncle Joe from the TV show 'Petticoat Junction') came in the store and said excitedly, 'Martha! They just found Mr Donahue in the river. Somebody hooked'im while they were fishin'!'

Aunt Madie quit shaking Jane, stood up and turned around to address Edgar. I thought maybe she was going to shake him, too, but she and Martha only followed him outside to see if any more news was running up the hill. I finally found the energy to slide off the stool and walk over to my bewildered and forgotten sister, who proceeded to tell me the details of how she hooked him ('I thought it was a log').

Mary Ellis, *Casting in the Fog: Reflections on a Fishing Siste*.

ANGLERS YOU WON'T MIND
MEETING ON THE RIVERBANK

The Oracle

The font of all angling wisdom, this fisher is often the most unassuming and ordinary guy on the bank. As they are becoming an increasingly rare find, you should cherish their company and absorb as much of their vast knowledge as you can when you meet them. You will know when you come across an Oracle, as half your day will be gone in deep conversation yet you never think begrudgingly of this lost time. Oracles exhibit a fair degree of eccentricity. They have a complete inability to remember the time and cannot for the life of them operate a mobile phone; however, there is a degree of sagely confidence to their fishing, which leaves most of us for dead.

THE ONES THAT GOT AWAY

Some fish are territorially beyond the reach of even the most determined fishermen. Those that dwell in the dark canyons of the deepest ocean beds are almost impossible to catch, and the specimens that have been rounded up by submarines have often exploded with the pressure change. Here are a few of them, and their freakish physical attributes:

Bristlefish
(Long and snakelike, with a line of glowing dots on its underside)

Deep sea angler fish
(Similar to shallower-dwelling species, but with much nastier teeth)

Black swallower
(Distensible stomach that can become bigger than the rest of its body)

Stoplight loosejaw
(The only creature in the world with a flashing red light on its head)

SAVING THE GWYNIAD

As you have probably already realised, the gwyniad is a fish of Welsh origin and a very rare one at that. To date, there is only one lake in North Wales left with a population of this unique herring-like species. The poor gwyniad has, in the past, been fished down almost to the point of extinction by netsmen eager to sell them as food. Now scientists are trying to reverse the decline and have set about conserving the remaining fish by trying to establish a separate population in a nearby lake. Rather than physically moving the endangered adult fish, they have been planting out fertilised eggs into the new water in the hope that some fish will grow on and establish new shoals of gwyniad.

YOU WEIR IT WELL

In Wales one of the earliest forms of fishing was not with rod and line, but by making a 'weir'. A small wall or dam would be made either from stones or wooden sticks and this would be placed across the river once a good head of migratory fish like salmon and trout had run upstream. The weir effectively trapped the fish in the shallows without any means of escape. It would then simply be a case of every man for himself, as the hapless fish were jumped on and speared either with a crude harpoon or a three-pronged trident. In Scotland, similar early methods of fish catching are known as 'cruives', whereas in England the ancient fishermen simply referred to them as 'fish dams' or 'traps'.

A BIT FISHY

Which fish was called the nurse fish because
of its supposed medicinal powers?
Answer on page 153.

WHAT ANGLERS SUFFER IN
THE NAME OF THEIR SPORT

Castinear-itus
This is a painful ailment normally associated with the fly fisher. That prize fish always seems just out of reach, and in one superhuman effort the angler will try and launch his line just that little bit further. At precisely the same moment a gust of wind strikes and instead of going that extra yard the fisher hooks his ear and goes the extra mile to outpatients to have the hook of the fly removed under local anaesthetic.

EXPLODING TOADS

In April 2005 anglers enjoying a little evening fishing on a lake near Hamburg were startled by loud pops and bangs near the waters edge. The source of the explosions turned out to be toads which have developed a defence mechanism of puffing themselves up to bloated size in a bid to fend off predatory crows. Unfortunately the toad's defences seem to have gone completely haywire and the toad effectively blows itself up before dying a messy death in the undergrowth. Environmentalists have been called in to try and find out if anything can be done to stop the toads exploding, but since bacterial or viral water born infection has already been ruled out it looks as if the cause will remain a mystery for the time being.

Women! Never here when you need 'em.

A LITERARY CATCH

First of all, the biggest mistake any angler can make is to be too successful. The 'Brotherhood of the Angle' – a concept much beloved of angling writers of a bygone age (may they rest in peace) – is unfortunately a myth. Human frailty exists in all men, whether they are financiers or philanderers, artists or anglers. And in angling, as in business, art or love, jealousy is seldom absent. Regrettable though it may be, some anglers cannot bear to see another catching more fish than they catch themselves. And if his success derives from the use of an unusual method – even though it be merely a variation of an old theme – the presumptuous innovator can be sure that the 'sporting' aspects of his method will soon come under attack. Indeed, on some fisheries the objectors, if they can make sufficient fuss, may even succeed in getting the method banned.

It is pointless to rail at such behaviour. The grizzlers have always existed and will always exist, and one would be naive to think that anything can be done to change them. Nevertheless, although they cannot be changed, they can and should be controlled. But they seldom are.

Falkus and Buller, *Freshwater Fishing*

*If the angler take fysshe surely thenne is
noo man merier in his spryte.*
Attributed to Dame Juliana Berners

KINGS AND COMMONERS

This is the story of two fish, both the same species but very different bedfellows. On the one hand there is the King of Fish, the wild salmon, a silver, sleek, well muscled creature genetically imprinted to navigate thousands of miles to feed off the coast of Greenland before returning to its British river home. Not only that but the Atlantic salmon has the capacity to remember exactly which river it was born in and will only migrate to and from its own unique stream to spawn. While at sea, the fish will studiously ignore any other 'strange' rivers, swim past them and make a beeline for their own home. Centuries of inherited gene power ensures that this amazing life cycle continues unbroken. That's what being a wild salmon is all about.

Compare this with what has become known as 'fake' salmon. These are farmed fish, lardy beasts bearing little resemblance to the real thing. How can the? They are grown from birth in a tank and forced to swim round and round forever in tightly packed circles. They are fed on pellets stained with a special dye to make their flesh seem pink (it's white-grey because they never get to eat what wild salmon do). This is a salmon with all its journeyman genes missing. Because it's been born and bred in a cage, the homing urge just isn't there in these sad and rather pathetic fish.

But does this matter? Farmed fish are apparently still fairly nutritious and cheap even if they are a bit clueless. However, they now pose a huge threat to our dwindling stock of wild fish. Their poorly-sited sea cages frequently break open in Atlantic storms and the fish with the non-existent long-term memory escape to sea, where they mix and mingle with the smarter wild ones.

Some farmed fish may even try and mate with native female salmon and this could spell disaster for the already hard-pressed King of Fish. For if the daft ones spawn with the wild ones, ancient genetic lines will be severed in a stroke and the subsequent offspring will be 'mongrel' hybrids, incapable of doing what wild salmon have been doing for centuries. Which could mean a catastrophic end for an already, much exploited fish.

CHALLENGING FISHING GEMS
ACROSS THE UK

Every angler has some waters he or she would like to keep secret: special places where time is forgotten and the magic of fishing takes over completely. There follows a few recommendations for the avid game fisher who likes a challenge:

River Frome, *Dorset:*
A meandering gin clear chalkstream where golden gleams of big trout are glimpsed between waving ranunculus. Testing, comparatively inexpensive fly fishing for wary trout in beautiful Dorset.

River Nevern, *Pembrokeshire:*
Inspiring small spate river where sewin and salmon rush into dark tree lined pools. When the water is fining down after heavy rain this is the place to be in west Wales.

Lough Melvin, *Northern Ireland:* Enigmatic west coast Irish lough full of trout mysteries including the famed Gillaroo and Sonaghen as well as enormous Ferox. Difficult enigmatic water at times but a place which once discovered holds you in its spell.

River Tummel, *Perthshire, Scotland:* A demanding tributary of the bigger River Tay where trout, salmon and grayling hide themselves extremely well in clear gravely pools. A water that manages to be bewitching, beguiling and bloody minded all in one go.

Loch Watten, *Caithness Scotland:* This shallow and rich clear water loch just screams wild trout at you. A place to enjoy long drifts in the boat and watch the sun go down.

THE BOAT THAT I TOW

A humongous 322lb halibut hooked by a sea angler off the Norwegian coast proved too heavy to land in his 30ft boat. Fortunately he had put to sea with an industrial-sized engine which, when run at full throttle, enabled the surprised but happy angler to literally tow the live catch back to the harbour. He then netted a tidy sum by selling it to a local fish-processing plant. At least he was able to tow his catch to land; anglers fishing from light rowing boats without an engine, sometimes find the tables completely turned. In 1998 a large salmon towed a rowing boat and its two occupants around on remote Loch Loyal in Sutherland for over half an hour before the fly eventually came loose and the fish escaped capture. Truly the one that got away.

RECYCLING YOUR FISHING LURES

Americans love their beer and their fishing, often, but not necessarily always, in that order. Now a company called www.bottlecaplure.com have come up with the ingenious idea of using all those spent bottle caps to catch fish. The company recycles the caps, flattens them out, reshapes them and then attaches a treble hook to fashion them into a spinning lure. Apparently the bottle cap lure has been very successful in catching a variety of fish species including walleye, salmon, trout, bass, char and perch. According to the manufacturer's website, angler Andy Vander Pleog has already won two consecutive National Championships using this new weapon. What it doesn't say is how much beer he drank in order to construct the lure.

IT'S A FACT

In 2005 the long-overdue formation of the Fisheries and Angling Conservation Trust (FACT) brought together many, otherwise disparate English-based fishing bodies under the one roof. Founder members include among others the Salmon and Trout Association, Angling Trades Association, Coarse Fisheries Association, National Association of Fisheries, Atlantic Salmon Trust and the National Federation of Sea Anglers. The move has been welcomed by anglers who see it as a positive move in presenting the case for angling in a more unified way. In the past fishing concerns have often been poorly presented, with anglers failing to speak with one accord.

By pooling resources in this way it is hoped that the interests of anglers and fisheries will be better represented in government circles.

FOODY FLIES

Olives

Banish any image of a trout rising to a cocktail stick impaled with a piquant Greek olive, perhaps spiked with a red dash of pimento. What fishermen are talking about here is an insect known as an 'olive'. These are upwinged flies related to the mayfly and when they hatch on a river or lake, trout feed on them avidly. Probably because olives are such a prolific British insect, some of the earliest flies ever made, which was somewhere around the fourteenth century, vaguely resembled olives with their prominent wing and dark body. Olives that the trout find tasty include the 'lake olive', 'medium olive', 'large dark olive', 'pond olive', 'rough olive' and 'blue winged olive'.

WHEN THE CANAL WON'T DO

Up until the 1970s, most British anglers were reasonably content to fish their local waters, and only a small minority headed for exotic destinations, with the sole purpose of fishing. Nowadays with increased leisure time, cheaper flights and greater spending power, anglers are venturing further afield. In 2005, these were just some of the fishing destinations being advertised:

Alaska • Australia
Bahamas • Baja
Belize • British Columbia
Canada • Christmas Island
Costa Rica • Cuba
Denmark • Egypt
Florida • Greenland • Holland
Iceland • India
Kamchatka • Kenya
Kola Peninsula
Madeira • Mauritius
Mexico • Mongolia
Montana, USA
Namibia • Nepal
Newfoundland • New Zealand
Norway • Patagonia • Peru
Russia • Sardinia
Seychelles • South Africa
Spain • Sweden • Slovenia
Thailand • Venezuala

SEA TROUT PIONEERS

Sir Herbert Maxwell

Sea trout fishing in the UK enjoys almost cult status, and with good reason – it has always been an incredibly difficult branch of game angling to get exactly right. This is due as much to the fickle secretive nature of the fish as it is to the anglers' skill. But Sir Herbert Maxwell, an eminent nineteenth-century scientist, was one of the first to define the techniques necessary for successful sea trout angling, which he outlined in his book *Salmon and Sea Trout*, published in 1898. Among other things, he was the first to acknowledge sea trout as a separate species, albeit by misnaming them 'salmon trout'. These fish, he declared, were different from Atlantic salmon and therefore the angler might need to use different techniques to fish for them. Prior to Maxwell's book, the sea trout was not much recognised as anything other than a pest that got in the way of salmon angling.

FAMOUS LADIES IN FISHING

Miss Ballantine

In September 1922 Georgina Ballantine hooked a huge salmon of 64lb on the Glendelvine beat of the River Tay. Two hours later she landed it, albeit with a fair bit of advice and encouragement from her father, an experienced gillie, who was in the boat with her. To his credit he did not once take over the rod from his daughter and though she suffered aching arms for days after, with this momentous catch she propelled herself forever into salmon fishing history. Eighty-three years later the record has never been broken.

TROUT FAVOURITES

Trout fishers across the UK have a selection of flies they would never leave home without. Here are a dozen stalwarts which rarely fail:

Bibio
Black (or brown) hoppers
Black gnats
Black pennel
Bumbles
Butcher
Great red sedge
Greenwells glory
Hares ear
Invicta
Soldier palmer
Zulu

AND HERE IS THE NEWS

In 2005, fishing-related news snippets garnered from the French website www.sea-river.com featured the following ground shakers; apparently in France, the numbers of fish species including salmon, shad and lamprey passing through fish counters at the dams at Vichy, Mauzac and Chatelleraut increased considerably in 2004. Both gourmets and anglers are rejoicing over this, though with typical 'Je ne sais quoi' style they declare they know little or nothing as to the cause of this improvement. The internet site also reports that in the UK the Brits are now consuming Prozac albeit unwittingly in their tap water, while in Italy it records that the town council of Monza has decided to ban the keeping of fish in round bowls. According to an Italian official for the environment, the fish are suffering because they have a distorted view of reality.

FISHING FOR LOBSTERS

In the early 1960s, when lobsters were more prolific off the west coast of Scotland than they are today, local children used to tempt a few from their lairs by the following method:

Take one strong garden cane, one thin wire coat hanger (the bronze ones are best), garden twine, a thick bath towel, plenty of limpet bait, a few strong elastic bands and a pinch of patience. Position yourself on those big boulder rocks where natural little sea caves have formed underneath. What you want is clear water about three feet deep, well washed by the tide and not overly weedy. Straighten out the coat hanger, thread on the bait, bend the hanger into a loop shape and place the end into the stub of the cane. Tie on securely with the twine and then, keeping your shadow off the water, dangle the bait down between the rocks. Leave for a while and, if you are lucky, a lobster will cautiously crawl out to investigate.

Do not make any sudden movement or touch the cane at this point or the big crustacean will take flight faster than you can say 'seine nets'. Hold your nerve and let him secure his big nippers round the bait and start to drag it back to his lair. Then with a lightening-fast wrist-flick, whisk up the clinging lobster and dive on it with the bath towel. Wrap the towel round the scuttling angry beast as fast as you can – any hesitation and it's gone. With all haste, leg it with the squirming bundle back on to the beach as far away from the water as possible. If you can muster enough courage, grab hold of the angry crustacean at its back midsection where it cannot swing round and nip you, and with opened-out elastic bands on your other hand, slip them quickly over each claw.

Alternatively if nothing bites, sunbathe on the bath towel and take home a few soggy limpets instead.

HOW FISH GOT THEIR NAMES

Grayling

Ancient anglers who caught grayling noticed the fish have a light smell of the herb thyme about them, hence their Latin name *Thymallus*. Up until the late eighteenth century, the grayling was also known as the 'umber', meaning shadow, presumably a name derived from its dark secretive outline. 'The Lady of the Stream' is another handle for grayling first coined in the nineteenth century by esteemed English angler Francis Francis who said: 'If the trout be the gentleman of the streams, the grayling is certainly the lady.' The fish are relatively common across most of England, parts of Wales and as far north in Scotland as Perthshire.

*What do you mean, you dropped
my Hardy rod over the side?*

QUOTE UNQUOTE

*A fishing pole is a stick with a hook at
one end and a fool at the other.*
Samuel Johnson, author

SAYINGS WITH A VAGUELY FISHY THEME

We took the bait, widened our net, cast around for some ideas and
these are just a few of the well-hooked, fishy sayings we managed to
reel in and dredge up. Luckily we didn't fall for anything hook, line
and sinker but you can tell us to put an oar in it if you like. Or you
could just let us off the hook...

Taken the bait
Widened the net
Dredged it up.
Let off the hook
Well hooked
Cast around for ideas
Caught in the net
Reeled it in
Put an oar in it
Swallowed it, hook line and sinker

All the things Papa wrote about the fight are true. There is not another strength as holy and unrestrained as the strength of that one beautifully mad fish. Once it is hooked, it will seek its freedom a thousand times before it gives up.

Before I had thought it was all foolishness, this man's business of fighting a fish. But it is not. There is luck involved in the testing of one life against another. And you do begin to love the fish because all the pain you are going through just to keep him on the line is equal to the pain he feels in his attempts to lose the thing that has gripped him.

I became nearly delirious after an hour and a half in the chair. The sun was high and there were no clouds or even a faint breeze. The wet towel was still on my head and countless buckets of seawater from the Gulf Stream had been poured over me. The salt had dried on my arms and I could taste the brine running down the parched back of my throat. I had a few sips of beer, a drag off a cigarette and a Fig Newton that Hilary had crammed into my mouth. My feet were cramping because I had to strain to reach the footplates on the fighting chair.

I kept trying desperately to find the horizon and some sign of the blue marlin that Tommy said weighed four hundred pounds and that was feeling heavier by the minute. But I wasn't seeing too well. There were silver spots floating before me and my heart was skipping beats.

Heatstroke. Sunstroke, I thought. Maybe just a good, old-fashioned sunstroke. I'll fall off this chair and never be able to walk again and then they'll be sorry for what they've put me through.

Lorian Hemingway,
The Young Woman and the Sea

ANGLING PLOYS THAT DIDN'T CATCH ON

Webster's loop rod

In the late 1800s a Scottish angler David Webster started to use a fishing rod that consisted of three pieces of wood spliced together. This was nothing out of the ordinary, but what made it different was the fact that instead of tying the fishing line to the top of the rod, the line was attached to a strong plaited loop of horsehair bound around the rod tip. This loop was, so Webster claimed, a boon to all fly fishers allowing for easy casting, and indeed he was very skilled with it. Unfortunately other anglers never got the hang of it, Webster's idea floundered in the twentieth century and the loop rod never took the place of the traditional fly rod.

REASONS TO GO FISHING

Anglers can always come up with an excuse to go fishing. Here are some of the better ones:

- You are engaged in research into fish species.
- The freezer is empty.
- You need fresh air.
- You just know you will catch that monster you missed last time.
- The pensioner next door has run out of fish.
- The dog needs the exercise.
- You want to test a new rod/reel/line/fly (rotate choice accordingly).
- You have an overwhelming desire to wear old clothes and truss yourself up in neoprene.
- Fishing is your hydrotherapy and anyway it's a lot cheaper than the spa.

A BIT FISHY

Which is the odd one out?
Truff, sprod, scurf, thorm, mort.
Answer on page 153.

BORDER ESK GOES ENGLISH

The fishing rights and ownership of the Border Esk River, which begins its life in Scotland but tips into the sea in England, have long been the cause of a bitter dispute between the two countries – for 550 years, in fact. Epic cross-border spats over salmon fishing have been going on since 1450. It seems that the English built a dam that trapped the salmon in their section of the river, effectively stopping any fish from reaching the Scottish half of the river. This led to endless rows and fights with not a little blood being shed over some 300 years before a rather inadequate compromise was reached which allowed some of the fish to swim upstream. In 2005 the Scottish Executive passed legislation allowing the English to demand a rod licence fee from anglers wanting to fish anywhere on the River Esk in both Scotland and England. Until this time in Scotland no rod licence had been necessary – only a permit fee was paid. This move has caused some nationalistic anglers with long memories to throw their hands up in horror; they say this is just another example of the English unfairly taking the lion's share. It would seem echoes of the '45 Rebellion loom large, even now ...

A FISHY DELIGHT

The trout of the UK are known to consume a varied diet of tasty morsels. These are just a few items regularly on the trout's menu:

Snails .
Freshwater shrimps
Beetles
Worms
Crayfish
Water louse
Limpets
Stonefly
Midges
Caddis fly
Mayfly
Sticklebacks
Small perch fry
Salmon eggs
Frogs and toads
Daddy long legs
Roach fry
Newts
Alder fly

QUOTE UNQUOTE

Yir juist aboot hauf an 'oor late wi yer striking.
Comment made to twentieth-century Scottish
angler W Robertson MD, by his gillie

ICEBERG AHOY

Antarctic fishing trawlermen collectively heaved a huge sigh of relief when in 2005 the drift of the world's largest iceberg, christened rather unimaginatively the 'B15-A', finally came to a halt. In late April it crashed into the Drygalski ice tongue with no casualties reported. Apparently this big bang, billed as 'the collision of the century', was supposed to happen some three months earlier. However, during January the icy colossus got stuck aground on a shallow sea mount.

This unexpected delay caused more upset by cutting off shipping routes than the eventual collision itself which was described by the head of the Oceans and Ice Unit as more like a bump in the night than the collision of the century.

A LITERARY CATCH

Allow your mind to become as one with the sound of the water and the wind in the trees. When you can observe and record without consciously seeing and hearing, instinct has begun to emerge. Don't be too sceptical. One day it may help you to fill your bag – as I am sure it helps those successful solitary fisherman, found on every river, who catch fish when others fail. This intuitive faculty is, I believe, an atavistic survival; a part of man's hunting instinct. Although it has been long submerged I feel certain that with help it can be brought to the surface. And I suggest that one way of doing this is to develop ones ability to see, read and understand the 'stories' of the countryside – a skill that must have been second nature to early man, but is now almost entirely forgotten. To do this we must learn to use our eyes and brains in a new way – or, rather, in a very old way: the way of our ancestral hunters.'

Hugh Falkus, *Sea Trout Fishing*

TOP TEN SALMON FLIES

All salmon anglers have their favourite flies – the ones they swear by when all else fails:

Allies shrimp
Blue charm
Garry dog
General practitioner
Munro killer
Silver doctor
Stoats tail
Thunder and lightning
Thunder stoat
Waddingtons

ANGLERS YOU MIGHT WANT TO AVOID

The Captain

Captains have seen military service or at least try hard to give that impression. They do everything in regimented fashion and hate any disruptions to routine like noisy children or small dogs. A typical fishing day will commence at 9.30am bang on, they stop for lunch exactly at 1pm and leave the water at 5pm precisely, fish activity or not. Captains are easily recognised by their back-slapping jollity, red faces and booming voices when their fishing has been productive. Equally they can be seen stamping around in furious temper blaming everyone else but themselves when they have failed to catch anything.

FAMOUS LADIES IN FISHING

Dame Juliana Berners

Dame Juliana was the principal (and the best known) editor of the very first British fishing book *The Treatise of Fishing with an Angle,* published in 1496. An educated, devout but sport-loving nun, she helped to bring together previously amassed fishing knowledge, both from European and British quarters. Though she is sometimes wrongly recorded as the sole author, the Dame must nevertheless be given huge credit in the assembling of this milestone work, which, 500 years on, remains at the pinnacle of fishing literature.

BLACK FISH

In 2005 two Shetland-based sea fishermen were found guilty of a fishing scam which had netted them nearly £3.5 million in illegal fish sales. By falsifying the log of the number of herring and mackerel landings they had made – declaring them within UK quota regulations while at the same time secretly unloading an extra 7,500 tonnes of 'black fish' in Danish ports – the skipper and his mate had over a two-year period enjoyed considerable wealth. Testimony to their success at fraud was seen in the form of their 12 million pound boat, Britain's biggest trawler, the Altaire. This boat, their main capital asset, has now been 'frozen' and legal proceedings are underway to reclaim the illegally generated cash, probably by selling this craft. It is thought that such is the stringency of EU regulations, up to 80% of the British fishing fleet now break EU fish quotas on a regular basis by selling their catch in other European ports but not declaring the proceeds to the authorities. Black fishing indeed...

FOODY FLIES

Eels

Europeans have consumed freshwater eels for centuries, but the particular type of eel that the fly fisher likes to imitate is the saltwater sand eel. These little eels, only about two or three inches long, form the staple diet of the sea trout as well as other oceanic fish. Despite over-exploitation of these fish, mainly by Danish trawlers who scoop them up by the tonne, they are still found in secluded sandy estuaries around the British coastline. Anglers fashion the sand eel fly from glittery fibres, tinsel and shiny paint and they mainly come in olive green, light blue and silver and are a remarkably good imitation of the real sand eel.

BIRDS OF A FEATHER

Ever since the first angler devised the first artificial fly, feathers have been an essential ingredient in their make up. These are just some of the birds that have supplied their plumage:

Blackbird
Cockerel
Mallard
Grouse
Hen
Peacock
Pheasant
Sea Gull
Starling
Teal

QUOTE UNQUOTE

Fishing is a laborious way of taking it easy.
Franklin P Jones, author

A LITERARY CATCH

By the time we had killed all the fish, and arranged them in rows to admire their beauty and size, the little captain (as the other men called him) subsided into a good humoured calm; and having offered a pinch of snuff to the gamekeeper, whom he generally fixed upon in particular to shout at, in consequence of a kind of rivalry between them, and also in consequence of his measuring some head and shoulders higher than himself, he made a brief apology for what he had said, winding it up by saying, 'And after all, that's no so bad, your Honour,' as he pointed to some giant trout; he then would light a pipe, and having taken a few whiffs, deliberately shove it alight into his waistcoat pocket, and extracting a netting needle and string, set to work mending any hole that had been made in the net. This done, and a dram of whisky having been passed round, the net was arranged on the stern of the boat, and they rowed round the wooded promontory to the other creek, keeping time to their oars with some wild Gaelic song, with a chorus in which they all joined, and the sound of which, as it came over the water of the lake, and died gradually away as they rounded the headland, had a most peculiarly romantic effect.

Charles St John,
Wild Sports of the Highlands

ALGAE AND ALZHEIMER'S

It has been known for some years that cyan bacteria, blue-green algae to you and me, are none too good for the digestive tract. If you drink water containing this algae you are likely to develop a stomach ache or much worse. This type of algae is regularly found in over-enriched waters, which suffer sewage and/or agricultural fertiliser pollution. Now in 2005 it seems that blue-green algae has also been linked to Alzheimer's disease. Apparently the algal blooms that occur in a number of lochs and lakes across Britain have been found to contain a neurotoxin, methyl-amino-ala-nine (BMAA) which can cause brain disease in humans. A team of international researchers, including scientists from Dundee University, have been researching the long-term effects of blue-green algae and have found that it acts as a slow neurotoxin and can cause symptoms identical to those of Alzheimer's. Yet another reason for not drinking untreated water. Falling into it also looks pretty risky.

A BIT FISHY

Which famous historical figure is thought to have died from a 'surfeit of lampreys'?
Answer on page 153.

SEA TROUT PIONEERS

Jeffrey Bluett

Jeffrey Bluett must be credited for rounding up the various sea trout angling theories of the first half of the twentieth century and conveying them all in practical fashion in his book *Sea Trout and Occasional Salmon* published in 1948. He firmly established night fishing as the most successful way of catching sea trout, and dispelled any anxieties that had troubled earlier writers about possible associations with salmon poaching (which also takes place at night). He advocated that anglers be flexible in their fishing tactics according to the changing weather conditions, which left the salmon-orientated dogma of the preceding years far behind. His descriptive powers were considerable, and few authors can beat his portrayal of sea trout activity in quiet river pools as the dawn breaks. He called it the 'crowded hour of glorious life' and made instant converts of many salmon anglers who were bored with catching little or nothing in the hard and bright days of July and August.

Number, times 10, of trout killed when untreated sewage was illegally discharged into the Brodiach Burn, near Aberdeen

ANGLING PLOYS THAT DIDN'T CATCH ON

Hollow butts

In the mid nineteenth century rods with hollow butt sections were made in Scotland. The idea of these was to store spare rod tips. The fine tips of the old fly rods were notoriously brittle and often broke while fishing. Rather than have to give up his sport, the angler could simply take out a replacement and attach it then and there. Unfortunately the hollow butt made the rod extremely difficult to cast with and the idea had to be dropped, although it was not entirely buried, as telescopic rods came into production in the 1960s.

SOME ESSENTIALS FOR THE FLY TYING KIT

You will find it difficult to tie a fly without the following:

A vice
Scissors
Tweezers
Spigot bobbin holder
Hackle pliers
Dubbing needle
Hooks
Threads
Wax
Tinsels
Feathers
Varnish
Dubbings (wool etc)
Fine wire

NELSON THE ANGLER

Not only was Admiral Nelson a legendary seafaring hero, but also he was apparently very skilled in wielding the fly rod. He spent most of his angling time upon the River Wandle, a famous chalkstream in his day but now sadly in need of restoration. Legend has it that he fished the river on the morning of the day he left to join his ship the Victory on 13 September 1805. Appropriately in 2005, the two-hundredth anniversary of Nelson's death, the Salmon and Trout Association launched fundraising efforts to help revive the fortunes of the River Wandle. Fundraising dinners were organised and all proceeds were put towards the Jet Set Club headed by Dr David Bellamy, which promotes the River Wandle Restoration Project.

WALK ON WATER

Anglers have always wanted to get to exactly where the fish are without the fuss of hiring a boat and carting with them all the paraphernalia that boat fishing attracts (oars, anchor, etc). In 2004 it seemed as if their prayers might have at last been answered. *The New York Times* reported that Yoav Rosen from Massachusetts had been granted a patent under the name 'Upright human floatation apparatus and propulsion mechanism' for an invention that allowed him to walk upright on water. Over 100 patents have been granted for water-walking apparatus in the last 150 years, but none of them has worked. Mr Rosen said that he had been working on the idea since he was 11 years old and had worked single-mindedly on various prototypes before coming up with what he saw as a winner.

Inspired by DaVinci's ideas for water walking which, according to models in the Leonardo Museum, look like a skier with two large floats on his feet using poles to keep him upright, Rosen had a similar but novel design. Gone are the ski poles, and the pontoons on the feet have flaps attached at the back to act like paddles. These flaps are light and buoyant and rotate from nine o'clock to 12 o'clock. The designer claims this makes them far superior to other inventions, which feature a six o'clock to nine o'clock rotation and allows the water walker to travel with some speed across the water surface. If the product ever gets off the ground – Rosen admits that, at the moment, 'it doesn't fit into an existing paradigm for sports' – then anglers may be able to do away with boats and walk straight out to where the piscatorial prey might be lying. Mr Rosen tested most of his prototypes on the Charles River; just what the fish made of it is anybody's guess.

ANGLERS YOU MIGHT WANT TO AVOID

Tackle Man

Tackle Man is immediately identifiable by the amount of new and often very expensive fishing equipment dangling about his person. He (and it nearly always is a he) has hugely inflated expectations of what this tackle can do for his fishing skills equating cost with success. Annoyingly, Tackle Man will often drain you dry of local knowledge and then pass it on to his friends as if he already knew it all. He has little interest in learning about fish species but high interest in having better kit than everyone else. Unless you feel like grovelling for a chance to fish the expensive water that Tackle Man has just leased (give up now, you have no chance), he is best to avoid.

She's blown on that bloody porridge again.

QUOTE UNQUOTE

Fishing is a world created apart from all others.
Norman MacLean, author of *A River Runs Through It*

A LITERARY CATCH

Allow your mind to become as one with the sound of the water and the wind in the trees. When you can observe and record without consciously seeing and hearing, instinct has begun to emerge. Don't be too sceptical. One day it may help you to fill your bag – as I am sure it helps those successful solitary fisherman, found on every river, who catch fish when others fail. This intuitive faculty is, I believe, an atavistic survival; a part of man's hunting instinct. Although it has been long submerged I feel certain that with help it can be brought to the surface. And I suggest that one way of doing this is to develop ones ability to see, read and understand the 'stories' of the countryside – a skill that must have been second nature to early man, but is now almost entirely forgotten. To do this we must learn to use our eyes and brains in a new way – or, rather, in a very old way: the way of our ancestral hunters.'

Hugh Falkus, *Sea Trout Fishing*

HOW FISH GOT THEIR NAMES

Bream

Bream are silvery, iridescent freshwater fish with either bluish or brownish backs that can be found in lakes and slow-going rivers all over the world. Many examples of 'sea-bream' also exist, their family name *Sparidae* accounting for at least 40 species in the globe's more exotic climes. It is likely that these tropical bream were named for much the same reason as their freshwater brethren – because of their spectacularly lustrous scales. From the proto-Germanic base word 'brehwan' meaning 'to shine, glitter or sparkle', came the West Germanic 'brasm', before being lengthened to the Frankish 'brahisma', and then shortened again to the Old French 'bresme' – the word from which its current pronunciation is derived.

THE FISHER AND THE SONG

We Gotta Get Out Of This Plaice, The Animals
Every ling I Do I Do For You, Bryan Adams
Day Bream Believer, The Monkeys
What If Cod Was One Of Us, Joan Osbourne
Almost Pike Being In Love, Nat King Cole
Hake On Me, Aha
Pike A Virgin, Madonna
Take Me Trout, Franz Ferdinand
Big Kipper, Elton John
It's A Fin, Pet Shop Boys
I Don't Want To Miss A Ling, Aerosmith
Blenny Rivers To Cross, Joe Cocker
Twist And Trout, The Beatles

SUPERSTITIONS OF THE SEAFARERS

Unlucky salmon

Despite being one of the most lucrative catches at sea, salmon were considered by many seafarers to be an unlucky fish. Superstitious fishers in the North of Scotland would always refer to the King of fish as 'the red fish' rather than its true name. If a salmon was found on board a boat, this spelled disaster and its discovery would prevent the fishermen from setting sail that day. Quite why this strange fear of salmon grew up has been lost in antiquity. It is doubly strange considering the symbolic links that Scottish salmon had with various cities in earlier times and the fact that they often appear in coats of arms.

TERRIBLE FISHING JOKES

Q. What is the fastest fish in the water?
A. A motopike.

Q. What is the difference between a fish and a piano?
A. You can't tuna fish.

Q: Why did the salmon cross the road?
A: Because it was tied to the chicken.

Q: Where do fish keep their money?
A: In the river bank.

Q. Why are fish so smart?
A. Because they swim in schools!

Q: What is the best way to talk to a fish?
A: Drop it a line.

FISHY PROVERBS

1. There's no plaice like home.
2. A fish in the hand is worth two in the lake.
3. Birds of a feather make flies.
4. A minnow is known by the company it keeps.
5. Make hake while the sun shines.
6. Don't look a pike horse in the mouth.
7. If you can't stand the haddock, stay out the kitchen.
8. There is more than one way to skin a cod.
9. The proof of the gudgeon is in the eating.
10. Nothing hurts like the weever.

WHAT ANGLERS SUFFER IN THE NAME OF THEIR SPORT

Caster's Whip

An involuntary spasm displayed by experienced anglers, Caster's Whip arises from years, or even decades, of practice devoted to perfecting a sound casting-action. Some way into a healthy and productive angling career, the process of flinging one's arm forth in a lithe, yet powerful, motion has ingrained itself into the muscle-memory a little too deeply. This then leads to instances of social embarrassment such as spontaneously belting members of the public in queues, giving a misleading image of the angler's personality, or showering barmen with beer at the local. Neither case allows much room for explanation. In the former, the angler will be pursued through the streets in a frantic, Benny Hill-style chase; in the latter, he will invariably be told: 'You're barred.'

I was alcoholic then. I am now. But then I drank and called it heritage. Now I do not and call it grace.

What I did not understand back in 1980, when I was nobly trying to keep up the Hemingway drinking image, was that my grandfather was debilitated by drinking and that it was indeed the major contributing factor to his suicide. Hemingway scholars argue with me over this, believing in the superhuman myth and the man. But I understand the pain and degradation my grandfather endured when his drinking began to destroy his talent, his health. It is the one thing we truly had in common, and not one I need pretend to. And this understanding allows me compassion for a man who bore the necessary cross of being human and for the young woman in the story who had not yet recognised the dimensions of her own cross. There have been changes, too, in my views of big game fishing. All too often it is wholesale slaughter, fish taken for prize money in big game tournaments, and I cannot participate in the slow and certain decimation of these fish populations. As a woman who fishes, I have forsaken this arena of big game fish, partly because I have caught and released marlin, tarpon, shark and barracuda, I find it more enjoyable to spend time on a lake or in a trout stream. The physical energy is not as great, and the conscience rests easier.

And there is also nothing left to prove. Maybe there never was. If I proved anything it was that ghosts and legends grow beyond their boundaries into powers great enough to consume those who take them on. But I have freedom now from this business of legends. Caught and released, in a way.'

Lorian Hemingway, *The Young Woman and the Sea*

SEA TROUT PIONEERS

Hamish Stewart

The early half of the twentieth century saw a sudden burst of literature relating to the previously much ignored sea trout. Leading the way was Scottish angler Hamish Stewart with his *The Book of the Sea Trout* published in 1917. Stewart pushed back the barriers on how to fish for sea trout, declaring that the fish should be sought after in brackish water estuaries as well as up river and that they responded well to traditional brown trout flies. Prior to Stewart's observations, few bothered to fish exclusively for sea trout and those who did just whacked on a large salmon fly and left it at that, or simply caught sea trout by accident when salmon fishing. To these anglers, Stewart's book was a revelation.

And we have lift off..

QUOTE UNQUOTE

Fishing is a delusion entirely surrounded by liars in old clothes.
Don Marquis, New York newspaper columnist and author

ANGLERS YOU WON'T MIND MEETING ON THE RIVERBANK

The Spear-fisher

A wiry and feral breed of angler, the Spear-fisher is an uncommon sight on many British waterways – the few we can lay claim to having emerged only as a result of watching too many re-runs of Tom Hanks in *Cast Away*. As the *Cast Away* cult took its form, members of this strange subculture were compelled to relinquish material possessions, commune with basketballs for spiritual fulfilment and, of course, run fish through at lightning speed with lethal, home-made spears. Given the general lack of remote tropical coasts around Britain, the Spear-fishers took to their local rivers, where they can be seen wading up to their ankles in the shallows, peering into the water and waiting with point-blank precision to strike. Spear-fishers consider it rude to be interrupted mid-hunt, in case they spear their own feet by accident. But, approached politely, they will stop pretending that they're lost and alone on an unknown grid-reference and happily teach strangers the art – an alternative to all that new-fangled business with rods and lines and stuff.

SUPERSTITIONS OF THE SEAFARERS

The albatross

Perhaps the godfather of all sailors' hang-ups, the albatross has long been regarded as a harbinger of bad weather. But a glance beneath the feathers of that symbolic meaning reveals a whirlpool of mysticism. In Amicale Internationale des Capitaines au Long Cours Cap Horniers (AICH) – a group of sailing veterans who have successfully steered ships around the perilous Horn – are dubbed 'albatross', in honour of their good fortune. In December 1992, the association's memorial was inaugurated in Chile. It is etched with a poem by Sara Vial of Valparaíso, which begins: 'I, the albatross that awaits at the end of the world... I am the forgotten soul of the sailors lost...' The point being that, among seafarers, albatrosses are regarded as reincarnations of sailors who have drowned at sea. And with an estimated 10,000 seamen lost to the Horn's watery grave, if Samuel Taylor Coleridge's *Rime of the Ancient Mariner* is true, it really would be double the injustice to kill one.

QUOTE UNQUOTE

Of all the maddening things, the worst is falling into the water.
H Plunkett Greene, twentieth-century author

A LITERARY CATCH

Should it be a good Mayfly season it is perfectly marvellous in what multitudes that insect appears. On the Kennet or Test or Itchen, or even on the Derbyshire Wye, the very air is thick with them, while the rivers are covered by their bodies, dead or alive. Where the Great Western Railway runs close to the Kennet I have seen the inside of a carriage absolutely teeming with them, somewhat to the consternation of a friend of mine who was not well acquainted with the habits of this insect. When the fly is thickly 'up' it is almost comic to watch the efforts of the small birds yet one more. They sit on branches, and literally gasp, so full are they of the succulent food. I am bound to say they do their little best in this direction, instinct doubtless teaching them that but a short ten days can be counted on wherein to revel in their rare dainty. In fine, brief though it may be, the Mayfly season is one which, coming as it does when the country is in the first and best bloom of its beauty, must always appeal strongly to the feelings of any fisherman.

Marquess of Granby and others,
Feather and Fin Series – The Trout

SEA TROUT PIONEERS

RC Bridgett

Scottish angler RC Bridgett advanced the difficult art of sea trout angling into the twentieth century. His book *Sea Trout Fishing* published in 1929 was one of those rare works that managed to be philosophical and practical at the same time. He has gone down in history as being one of the first anglers to acknowledge the need to fish for sea trout at night with large black flies sunk deep in the river flow. However, he had to be careful when advocating this method, as the salmon poacher also operates at night and Bridgett did not want any association to be made between the bona fide sea trout fisher and those with less than honourable intent.

ALT TOGETHER NOW

In the Gaelic language, a river or burn in Scotland is usually known as 'alt', which is sometimes corrupted to 'ault'. This prefix is often assimilated into place names. Here's a few:

Altnaharra • Altnabreac • Altandhu
Altnacreig • Altass • Aultbea
Ault a'chruinn • Aultguish
Aultmore • Aultnamain
Aultnagoire • Aultgrishin

FISH WARS

Icy stares across the Med

In mid-June 2003, a Spanish armed patrol boat intercepted a Moroccan fishing vessel 37 miles off the coast of Lanzarote. It was the only one of three Moroccan crafts sighted that morning to be apprehended. Its crew comprised of 15 Moroccans and four Spanish chancers, and its hold contained 4,500 kilos of fish and prawns. The crew told the unconvinced Spanish authorities that the catch was obtained in Moroccan waters. This incident was merely an addition to a long-running territorial dispute between Spain and Morocco, dating right back to Morocco's former status as a French and Spanish protectorate. Fishing disputes between the two countries have been traditionally bilateral, but more recently have been co-ordinated by the EU. As the only oil-free North African country, Morocco depends upon high seas fishing for economic survival, but the Spanish argue that this has led it to dip into their waters far too often. To complicate matters, the countries have also tussled over the one kilometre-wide islet, Perejil, in the Straits of Gibraltar. It is, of course, totally uninhabited.

ANGLERS YOU MAY WANT TO AVOID

The Cagoule

Imagine a processed-cheese sandwich on white bread in human form, and you have the Cagoule. The fishing first-cousin of the civilian 'Anorak', he is often seen huddled on the bank wrapped up in an oversized, crinkly waterproof, clinging onto his rod and wondering what's gone so wrong in his life. As such he has known to wallow there for three days without a break – or a catch. Lacking any serious knowledge of the finer arts of fishing, the Cagoule comes to the river for want of other things to do. His paucity of skill leaves him with no alternative but to channel disenchantment down the fishing-line, in the hope that the fish will leap out of the water in order to avoid it. Sadly, this only drives them towards other anglers' hooks. Be warned: the Cagoule's voice can trigger off an existential crisis.

A FEW FISHY FILMS TO SEE

A Plaice in the Sun
Down and Trout in Beverley Hills
Gone with the Fins
Silence of the Clams
Gar Face
The Cod Father
Big Fish
The World According to Carp
The City of Cod
Bream Streets
Jack the Kipper
I Bream of Genie
Love is a Blenny Splendid Thing
Field of Breams
Some Pike it Hot

WHAT ANGLERS SUFFER IN THE NAME OF THEIR SPORT

Angler's Cramp

Angler's Cramp usually occurs after the preparatory stages of the day's activities, when all the lines have been tied, the flies fixed and the bait hooked. The condition strikes when the angler attempts to hurl his line into the water to find his casting arm firmly stuck behind his back. If the freeze extends to the angler's hand locking the rod at an awkward angle, it can be quite difficult to fit the patient into an ambulance, and firemen with cutting tools should be on hand to section the rod. Cod liver oil can help too.

DURING THE COMPILATION OF THIS BOOK,
THE COMPANION TEAM...

Gave up five days of prime salmon fishing on the
River Thurso, Caithness

Learned what a gillie does

Sampled the inspirational merits of various 12-year-old malts;
Cragganmore won by a short nose

Found out it was Stanley Unwin and not Stanley Mathews who was
the famous raconteur of nonsense rhymes in the 60's.
Stanley Mathews was a footballer

Promised Bea the Springer spaniel 42 long walks by the river, but
managed only 27

Discovered that sharks are not at all picky about what they eat

Found out there are a zillion different types of nets used in fishing

Consumed halibut, scallops, crab, herring and mackerel from
environmentally friendly North Sea trawlers

Exposed the secret life of a freshwater eel

Decided well-chilled Sancerre is absolutely 'the' best wine
to go with baked trout

Bought a whole bunch of new tackle items but have yet to use them

Found out the Gaelic for 'It got away'

*Please note that although every effort has been made to ensure
accuracy in this book, the above statistics may be the result
of brain-drain due to a spot of overfishing.*

A fish is too valuable to be caught only once.

Lee Wulff

The answers. As if you needed them.

P11. Redbelly tilapia, an Egyptian fish introduced to the UK, which has bred in the wild in Wales.

P18. They are used as bait to catch a bigger fish.

P29. Grouse. Its feathers are still used to construct certain types of fishing flies; the other birds' feathers are no longer used, as the birds are protected species.

P38. Trout. The colours all describe European trout except for the blue trout, which is a hybrid, a European trout cross-bred with an American rainbow trout.

P48. In a lake. This is the Latin name for a North American lake trout.

P53. They are all types of Irish char.

P64. The odd one out is houting, which is a white fish; all the others are obscure names for the allis shad.

P71. Whiting, herring, sparling, houting, whitling and ling (you could also have bitterling if you are really clever).

P80. These are different types of nymphs, which form a staple part of the diet of a trout.

P85. In fly fishing this was the forerunner of what is now known as 'false casting'. In the nineteenth century a fly could be dried in the air by a swishing cast known as the carshalton dodge.

P95. The wolf. There is a wolf fish and an American fly known as 'the grey wulff'.

P103. Roger Daltrey of The Who.

P112. He was the first angler in Europe to record fishing with an artificial fly instead of bait.

P116. Nineteenth-century salmon poachers based on the River Wye, southern England.

P125. The tench.

P135. The odd one out is thorm, which is made up; all the others are old colloquial names for the sea trout.

P140. King Henry I; the lampreys gave him ptomaine poisoning.

154 *Upper common weight in grammes for a smelt, also known as a sparling, found in UK waters*

FURTHER READING

Where to Fly Fish in Britain and Ireland, J Bailey
The Bright Stream of Memory, G Bucknall
Trout Fishers Handbook, L Crawford
Freshwater Fishing, Falkus and Buller
The Fly, A Herd,
Fishing and Thinking, AA Luce
A Dictionary of Fly Fishing, CB McCully
Where the Bright Waters Meet, Plunket Greene
Early Scottish Angling Literature, Professor NW Simmonds
The Wildlife Series – Trout, Edited by Stolz and Schnell

Number of recorded sites for the nine-spined stickleback in England 155
and Wales, since 1972

Just keep swimming.

Dory in the film *Finding Nemo*

ACKNOWLEDGEMENTS

We gratefully acknowledge permission to reprint extracts of copyright material in this book from the following authors, publishers and executors:

Casting in the Fog: Reflections on a Fishing Sister by Mary Ellis from *Uncommon Waters*, by permission of Seal Press.

Sea Trout Fishing by Hugh Falkus © HF & G Witherby 1962. This revised edition © Hugh Falkus 1975. Published by Cassell Illustrated. Reproduced by kind permission of the Estate of Hugh Falkus.

From *Freshwater Fishing* by Hugh Falkus and Fred Buller, published by Cresset Press. Reprinted by permission of The Random House Group Ltd.

From *Now I Lay Me*. Reprinted with permission of Scribner, an imprint of Simon & Schuster Adult Publishing Group, from *The Short Stories of Ernest Hemingway*. Copyright 1927 by Charles Scribner's Sons. Copyright renewed 1955 by Ernest Hemingway. Extract from *Now I Lay Me* from *Men Without Women* by Ernest Hemingway, published by Jonathan Cape. Reprinted by permission of The Random House Group Ltd.

The Young Woman and the Sea by Lorian Hemingway from *Uncommon Waters*, by permission of Seal Press.

The Birderman by Roger McGough from *Waving at Trains* (Copyright © Roger Mcgough 1982) is reproduced by permission of PFD (www.pfd.co.uk) on behalf of Roger McGough.

Where the Bright Waters Meet, Harry Plunket Greene, published by Andre Deutsch, reproduced by permission of Andre Deutch Limited, part of the Carlton Publishing Group.

Saturday Night and Sunday Morning, Alan Sillitoe © 1958, by permission of HarperCollins Publishers Ltd.

INDEX

Alaska 22, 30, 59, 130

Angling authors 13, 14, 19, 20, 26, 31, 34, 40, 43, 44, 52, 55, 57, 64, 65, 70, 71, 73, 75, 79, 83, 87, 90, 108, 113, 119, 123, 126, 127, 134, 137, 138, 139, 143, 146

Antipodes 41, 71, 84, 109, 130

Bait 20, 31, 39, 41, 47, 48, 59, 61, 63, 66, 70, 74, 79, 92, 96, 99, 104, 108, 118, 133

Bass 10, 27, 55, 66, 97, 108, 116, 122, 129

Bastard, Thomas 61

Berners, Dame Juliana 56, 58, 75, 113, 127, 138

Bream 51, 144

Bridget, RC 75

Buchan, John 48

Burton, Robert 96

Carp 39, 48, 55, 96, 110

Casting 14, 40, 75, 79, 81, 100, 104, 125, 133, 141, 145, 150

Caspian Sea 32

Catfish 33, 55

Chalkstreams 32, 76, 128, 141

Char 30, 44, 96, 129

Churchill, Winston 121

Coarse fishing 14, 34, 37, 46, 48, 61, 63, 117, 118

Cod 15, 25, 51, 71, 79, 84, 95, 112, 121, 122, 144, 145

Coelacanth 38

Coleridge, Samuel Taylor 47, 148

Crabbe, George 81

Cyberfishing 27, 71, 72, 83

Darwin, Charles 86

Davenant, Sir William 91

Dogfish 15, 47

Ecology 10, 17, 19, 22, 23, 28, 32, 34, 70, 85, 92, 106, 107, 113, 121, 122, 124, 129, 131, 138, 140

Eel 15, 47, 70, 95, 111, 112, 118, 119, 122, 138

Celebrity anglers 50

Female anglers 37, 56, 82, 110, 123

Fish biology 15, 74, 93, 95, 97, 101, 107, 109, 118, 121, 122

Fish cuisine 30, 37, 108, 111, 112, 113, 117

Fish predators 78, 89, 102

Fisher, Nick 84

Fishing disputes 10, 19, 24, 32, 50, 135, 149

Fishing folklore 11, 12, 44, 45, 75, 82, 95, 109

Fishing innovations 25, 27, 43, 51, 54, 59, 78, 80, 98, 125, 134, 141, 142

Fly fishing 14, 17, 18, 22, 27, 28, 29, 34, 35, 39, 40, 42, 46, 52, 55, 61, 64, 65, 66, 68, 69, 76, 77, 81, 82, 88, 91, 92, 94, 96, 100, 102, 103, 107, 116, 117, 120, 128, 129, 131, 134, 135, 137, 138, 139, 141

Floats 14, 27, 47, 49, 54, 61, 71, 79, 99

Game fishing 19, 25, 26, 42, 46, 71, 86, 119, 128, 146

Goldfish 29, 33, 112, 117

Grayling 132

Gudgeon 41, 63, 107, 145

Haddock 15, 25, 51, 145

Halford, FM 40

Heraldry 10, 97

Herring 15, 25, 25, 47, 53, 96, 112, 138

Hirst, Damien 17

Hooks 20, 42, 49, 59, 68, 72, 102, 133, 141

Hunt, James Henry Leigh 83

Influential anglers 56, 76, 90

Ireland 70, 84

James, Henry 39

Jaws 25

Jaws Two, 122

Jerome, Jerome K 58

Johnson, Samuel 133

Kingsley, Charles 51
Knots 62, 68
Lines 14, 18, 26, 34, 42, 46, 55, 59, 61, 63, 71, 73, 78, 80, 81, 85, 96, 103, 104, 118, 121, 125, 133, 135, 145
Lobster 132
Mackerel 15, 59, 70, 112, 138
Marine Protected Areas 19
Marlin 71, 74
Mayflies 16, 119, 136, 148
McGough, Roger 104-5
Melly, George 73
Nets 18, 46, 49, 80, 103, 113, 124, 133
Otter 111
People for the Ethical Treatment of Animals (PETA) 103
Peterson, Professor Jack 27
Pike 30, 36, 57, 70, 112, 116, 144, 145
Porpoise 15, 106
Purism 40
Ransome, Arthur 65
Rare fish 82
Reels 25, 47, 49, 59, 73, 78, 81, 133, 135
Robertson MD, W 136
Rods 14, 19, 30, 34, 46, 47, 49, 59, 60, 73, 75, 78, 80, 82, 83, 85, 92, 118, 125, 134, 135, 141
Saithe 47, 71, 92
Salmon 12, 15, 20, 22, 26, 29, 34, 45, 46, 48, 57, 61, 62, 71, 79, 84, 85, 86, 87, 88, 92, 94, 96, 109, 110, 112, 114, 117, 120, 121, 122, 124, 127, 128, 129, 130, 131, 135, 136, 137, 140, 141, 144, 146
Scent 46
Schwarzenegger, Arnold 19
Scotland 10, 12, 16, 17, 19, 25, 29, 40, 48, 57, 69, 75, 77, 88, 89, 92, 114, 120, 128, 132, 135, 146, 149

Sea fishing 12, 17, 32, 36, 46, 50, 65, 66, 69, 70, 136, 137, 140, 146, 149
Seahorse 91
Seal 15, 78
Shark 15, 17, 58, 84, 95, 106, 122
Shakespeare, William 20, 71, 74
Shetland 119
Shrimp 29, 64, 112, 136
Silletoe, Alan 99
Skues, GEM 22
Spear fishing 71, 147
Squid 47, 79
Stewart, WC 65, 68, 94
Stevenson, Robert Louis 68
Stoddart, Thomas 47
Superstitions 43, 65, 98, 120, 144, 148
Sutcliffe, Tom 16
Smith, JLB 38
Swordfish 51, 74, 122
Taxidermy 21
Thoreau, Henry David 115
Travler, Ailm 59
Trout 10, 11, 17, 18, 19, 20, 21, 24, 27, 28, 32, 34, 35, 40, 43, 45, 57, 58, 63, 64, 66, 67, 68, 69, 78, 79, 81, 91, 92, 93, 94, 95, 96, 101, 103, 108, 112, 116, 117, 119, 123, 125, 128, 129, 130, 131, 136, 137, 140, 141, 144, 146, 148, 149
Tuna 25, 51, 74, 119, 145
Twain, Mark 55
Useful web addresses 32, 35, 39, 66, 82, 85, 92, 129, 131
Wales 21, 69, 124, 125
Walleye pollack 30, 47, 55, 59, 62
Waterway authorities 41, 50, 92, 110, 121, 129
Weather 45, 72
Weever 94
Whale 15, 95
Wild Trout Trust 32
Wotton, Henry 28

The Birdwatcher's Companion Twitchers, birders and ornithologists are all catered for in this unique book. ISBN 1-86105-833-0

The Cook's Companion Foie gras or fry-ups, this tasty compilation is an essential ingredient in any kitchen. ISBN 1-86105-772-5

The Countryside Companion From milking stools to crofters tools, this book opens the lid on the rural scene. ISBN 1-86105-918-3

The Fishing Companion This fascinating catch of fishy facts offers a whole new angle on angling. ISBN 1-86105-919-1

The Gardener's Companion For anyone who has ever gone in search of flowers, beauty and inspiration. ISBN 1-86105-771-7

The Golfer's Companion From plus fours to six irons, here's where to find the heaven and hell of golf. ISBN 1-86105-834-9

The History of Britain Companion All the oddities, quirks, origins and stories that make our country what it is today. ISBN 1-86105-914-0

The Ideas Companion The stories behind the trademarks, inventions, and brands that we come across every day. ISBN 1-86105-835-7

The Legal Companion From lawmakers to lawbreakers, find out all the quirks and stories behind the legal world. ISBN 1-86105-838-1

The Literary Companion Literary fact and fiction from Rebecca East to Vita Sackville-West. ISBN 1-86105-798-9

The London Companion Explore the history and mystery of the most exciting capital city in the world. ISBN 1-86105-799-7

The Moviegoer's Companion Movies, actors, cinemas and salty popcorn in all their glamorous glory. ISBN 1-86105-797-0

The Politics Companion Great leaders and greater liars of international politics gather round the hustings. ISBN 1-86105-796-2

The Sailing Companion Starboards, stinkpots, raggie and sterns – here's where to find out more. ISBN 1-86105-839-X

The Shakespeare Companion A long, hard look at the man behind the moustache and his plethora of works. ISBN 1-86105-913-2

The Traveller's Companion For anyone who's ever stared at a plane and spent the day dreaming of faraway lands. ISBN 1-86105-773-3

The Walker's Companion Ever laced a sturdy boot and stepped out in search of stimulation? This book is for you. ISBN 1-86105-825-X

The Wildlife Companion Animal amazements and botanical beauties abound in this book of natural need-to-knows. ISBN 1-86105-770-9